Science Notebook

for

Earth Science

Glencoe Science

Consultant

Douglas Fisher, Ph.D.

D1572785

Glencoe

New York, New York   Columbus, Ohio   Chicago, Illinois   Woodland Hills, California

About the Consultant

Douglas Fisher, Ph.D., is a Professor in the Department of Teacher Education at San Diego State University. He is the recipient of an International Reading Association Celebrate Literacy Award as well as a Christa McAuliffe award for Excellence in Teacher Education. He has published numerous articles on reading and literacy, differentiated instruction, and curriculum design as well as books, such as *Improving Adolescent Literacy: Strategies at Work* and *Responsive Curriculum Design in Secondary Schools: Meeting the Diverse Needs of Students*. He has taught a variety of courses in SDSU's teacher-credentialing program as well as graduate-level courses on English language development and literacy. He also has taught classes in English, writing, and literacy development to secondary school students.

The **McGraw·Hill** Companies

Send all inquiries to:
Glencoe/McGraw-Hill
8787 Orion Place
Columbus, Ohio 43240-4027

ISBN 0-07-874569-1

Printed in the United States of America

7 8 9   024   08 07

Table of Contents

Table of Contents

Note-Taking Tips

Your notes are a reminder of what you learned in class. Taking good notes can help you succeed in science. These tips will help you take better notes.

• Be an active listener. Listen for important concepts. Pay attention to words, examples, and/or diagrams your teacher emphasizes.

• Write your notes as clearly and concisely as possible. The following symbols and abbreviations may be helpful in your note-taking.

Word or Phrase	Symbol or Abbreviation		Word or Phrase	Symbol or Abbreviation
for example	e.g.		and	+
such as	i.e.		approximately	≈
with	w/		therefore	∴
without	w/o		versus	vs

• Use a symbol such as a star (★) or an asterisk (*) to emphasis important concepts. Place a question mark (?) next to anything that you do not understand.

• Ask questions and participate in class discussion.

• Draw and label pictures or diagrams to help clarify a concept.

Note-Taking Don'ts

• **Don't** write every word. Concentrate on the main ideas and concepts.

• **Don't** use someone else's notes—they may not make sense.

• **Don't** doodle. It distracts you from listening actively.

• **Don't** lose focus or you will become lost in your note-taking.

Using Your Science Notebook

This note-taking guide is designed to help you succeed in learning science content. Each chapter includes:

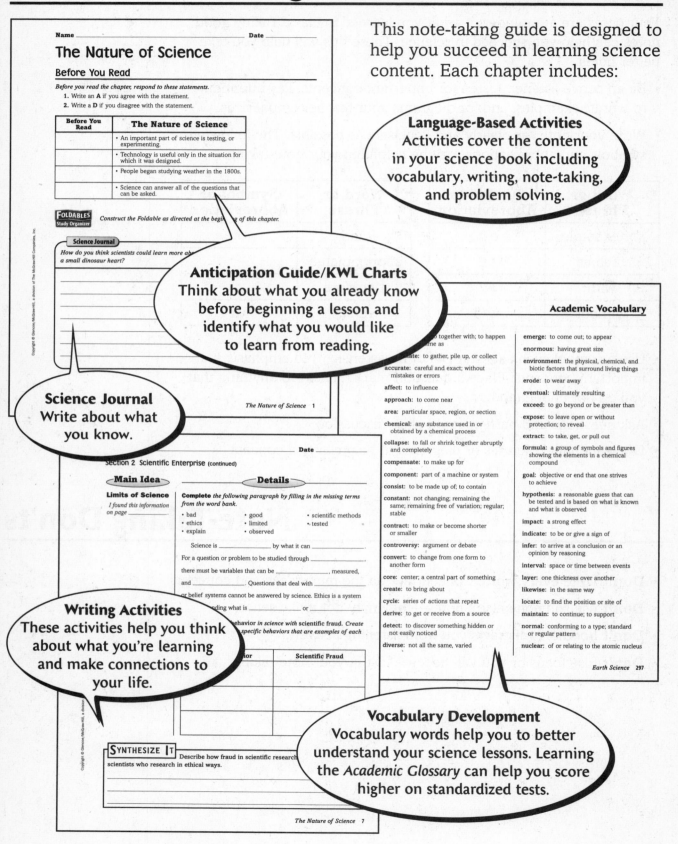

Language-Based Activities
Activities cover the content in your science book including vocabulary, writing, note-taking, and problem solving.

Anticipation Guide/KWL Charts
Think about what you already know before beginning a lesson and identify what you would like to learn from reading.

Science Journal
Write about what you know.

Writing Activities
These activities help you think about what you're learning and make connections to your life.

Vocabulary Development
Vocabulary words help you to better understand your science lessons. Learning the *Academic Glossary* can help you score higher on standardized tests.

Name _____ **Date** _____

The Nature of Science

Before You Read

Before you read the chapter, respond to these statements.
1. Write an **A** if you agree with the statement.
2. Write a **D** if you disagree with the statement.

Before You Read	The Nature of Science
	• An important part of science is testing, or experimenting.
	• Technology is useful only in the situation for which it was designed.
	• People began studying weather in the 1800s.
	• Science can answer all of the questions that can be asked.

FOLDABLES Study Organizer   *Construct the Foldable as directed at the beginning of this chapter.*

Science Journal

How do you think scientists could learn more about a small dinosaur heart?

The Nature of Science 1

Date _____

Section 2 **Scientific Enterprise** (continued)

Main Idea

Limits of Science

I found this information on page _____

Details

Complete *the following paragraph by filling in the missing terms from the word bank.*

- bad
- ethics
- explain
- good
- limited
- observed
- scientific methods
- tested

Science is _____ by what it can _____.

For a question or problem to be studied through _____, there must be variables that can be _____, measured,

and _____. Questions that deal with _____ or belief systems cannot be answered by science. Ethics is a system _____ing what is _____ or _____

_____ behavior in science with scientific fraud. *Create* specific behaviors that are examples of each

_____ior	Scientific Fraud

SYNTHESIZE IT   Describe how fraud in scientific research _____ scientists who research in ethical ways.

The Nature of Science 7

Academic Vocabulary

_____ together with; to happen _____ same as

_____ate: to gather, pile up, or collect

accurate: careful and exact; without mistakes or errors

affect: to influence

approach: to come near

area: particular space, region, or section

chemical: any substance used in or obtained by a chemical process

collapse: to fall or shrink together abruptly and completely

compensate: to make up for

component: part of a machine or system

consist: to be made up of; to contain

constant: not changing; remaining the same; remaining free of variation; regular; stable

contract: to make or become shorter or smaller

controversy: argument or debate

convert: to change from one form to another form

core: center; a central part of something

create: to bring about

cycle: series of actions that repeat

derive: to get or receive from a source

detect: to discover something hidden or not easily noticed

diverse: not all the same, varied

emerge: to come out; to appear

enormous: having great size

environment: the physical, chemical, and biotic factors that surround living things

erode: to wear away

eventual: ultimately resulting

exceed: to go beyond or be greater than

expose: to leave open or without protection; to reveal

extract: to take, get, or pull out

formula: a group of symbols and figures showing the elements in a chemical compound

goal: objective or end that one strives to achieve

hypothesis: a reasonable guess that can be tested and is based on what is known and what is observed

impact: a strong effect

indicate: to be or give a sign of

infer: to arrive at a conclusion or an opinion by reasoning

interval: space or time between events

layer: one thickness over another

likewise: in the same way

locate: to find the position or site of

maintain: to continue; to support

normal: conforming to a type; standard or regular pattern

nuclear: of or relating to the atomic nucleus

Earth Science 297

Name _____ Date _____

Section 1 Science All Around (continued)

‹Main Idea› **‹Details›**

Mysteries and Problems

I found this information on page _____

Summarize *why it was important for scientists to solve the mystery of the tsunami that struck Japan, on January 27, 1700.*

_____

_____

_____

_____

Scientific Methods

I found this information on page _____

Sequence *the scientific methods used to solve a scientific problem by completing the graphic organizer below.*

I found this information on page _____

_____ *specific*

1. _____   7. _____
2. _____   8. _____
3. _____   9. _____
4. _____   10. _____
5. _____   11. _____
6. _____   12. _____

The Nature of Science 3

Note-Taking Based on the Cornell Two-Column Format
Practice effective note-taking through the use of graphic organizers, outlines, and written summaries.

Chapter Wrap-Up
This brings the information together for you. Revisiting what you thought at the beginning of the chapter provides another opportunity for you to discuss what you have learned.

Name _____ Date _____

The Nature of Science Chapter Wrap-Up

Now that you have read the chapter, think about what you have learned and complete the table below. Compare your previous answers with these.

1. Write an **A** if you agree with the statement.
2. Write a **D** if you disagree with the statement.

The Nature of Science	After You Read
• An important part of science is testing, or experimenting.	
• Technology is useful only in the situation for which it was designed.	
• People began studying weather in the 1800s.	
• Science can answer all of the questions that can be asked.	

Review

Use this checklist to help you study.

☐ Review the information you included in your Foldable.

☐ Study your *Science Notebook* on this chapter.

☐ Study the definitions of vocabulary words.

☐ Review daily homework assignments.

☐ Re-read the chapter and review the charts, graphs, and illustrations.

☐ Review the Self Check at the end of each section.

☐ Look over the Chapter Review at the end of the chapter.

SUMMARIZE IT After reading ...
learned about the nature of sci...

8 *The Nature of Science*

Review Checklist
This list helps you assess what you have learned and prepare for your chapter tests.

Name _____ Date _____

Section 1 Science All Around (continued)

‹Main Idea› **‹Details›**

Working in the Lab

I found this information on page _____

Define *the four types of factors in a science experiment. Identify and describe each of them below.*

Independent Variable → [ ]

[ ] → variables that do not change

Dependent Variable → [ ]

[ ] → the standard to which results can be compared

Technology

I found this information on page _____

Summarize *transferable technology by defining the term. Then provide examples by filling out the graphic organizer below.*

Transferable technology is _____

_____

Radar and Sonar

originally developed for → [ ]

[ ] → are now used to study → [ ]

SYNTHESIZE IT Identify three objects in your home or school that have *not* been affected by technology.

_____

4 *The Nature of Science*

Graphic Organizers
A variety of visual organizers help you to analyze and summarize information and remember content.

The Nature of Science

Before You Read

Before you read the chapter, respond to these statements.

   1. Write an **A** if you agree with the statement.

   2. Write a **D** if you disagree with the statement.

Before You Read	The Nature of Science
	• An important part of science is testing, or experimenting.
	• Technology is useful only in the situation for which it was designed.
	• People began studying weather in the 1800s.
	• Science can answer all of the questions that can be asked.

Construct the Foldable as directed at the beginning of this chapter.

Science Journal

How do you think scientists could learn more about a clump of stone that could be a small dinosaur heart?

_____

_____

_____

_____

_____

_____

The Nature of Science
Section 1 Science All Around

Scan *Section 1 of your book, reading all section titles and bold words. Then write three facts that you have learned about the nature of science and scientific investigation.*

1. _____

2. _____

3. _____

Review Vocabulary

Define analyze *to show its scientific meaning.*

analyze

_____

New Vocabulary

Write a sentence that contains both terms from each pair.

hypothesis/control

_____

_____

scientific methods/
Earth science

_____

_____

variable/
independent variable

_____

_____

constant/
dependent variable

_____

_____

science/technology

_____

_____

Academic Vocabulary

Use a dictionary to define outcome *to show its scientific meaning.*

outcome

_____

Name _____ **Date** _____

Section 1 Science All Around (continued)

⟨ **Main Idea** ⟩	⟨ **Details** ⟩
Mysteries and Problems *I found this information on page* _____ .	**Summarize** *why it was important for scientists to solve the mystery of the tsunami that struck Japan, on January 27, 1700.* _____ _____ _____ _____
Scientific Methods *I found this information on page* _____ .	**Sequence** *the scientific methods used to solve a scientific problem by completing the graphic organizer below.*

┌────────────────────────────────┐
│   │
└────────────────────────────────┘
              ↓
┌────────────────────────────────┐
│   Gather information.   │
└────────────────────────────────┘
              ↓
┌────────────────────────────────┐
│   │
└────────────────────────────────┘
              ↓
┌────────────────────────────────┐
│   Test the hypothesis.   │
└────────────────────────────────┘
              ↓
┌────────────────────────────────┐
│   │
└────────────────────────────────┘
              ↓
┌────────────────────────────────┐
│   │
└────────────────────────────────┘

| **Science**

I found this information on page _____ . | **Distinguish** *topics that Earth scientists study by listing specific topics identified in this section.* |

1. _____   7. _____

2. _____   8. _____

3. _____   9. _____

4. _____   10. _____

5. _____   11. _____

6. _____   12. _____

Section 1 Science All Around (continued)

Main Idea ———————— **Details** ————————

Working in the Lab

I found this information on page _____ .

Define *the four types of factors in a science experiment. Identify and describe each of them below.*

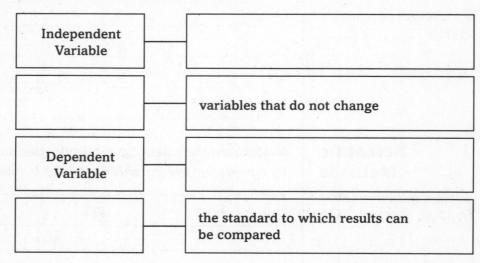

Independent Variable	
Define	variables that do not change
Dependent Variable	
	the standard to which results can be compared

Technology

I found this information on page _____ .

Summarize *transferable technology by defining the term. Then provide examples by filling out the graphic organizer below.*

Transferable technology is _____

_____ .

Radar and Sonar

originally
developed for

are now
used to
study

SYNTHESIZE IT Identify three objects in your home or school that have *not* been affected by technology.

_____

_____

The Nature of Science
Section 2 Scientific Enterprise

Skim *through Section 2 of your book. Write three questions that come to mind from reading the headings and examining the illustrations.*

1. _____

2. _____

3. _____

Review Vocabulary **Define** observation *to show its scientific meaning.*

observation _____

_____

New Vocabulary *Use your book to define the following terms.*

scientific theory _____

_____

scientific law _____

_____

ethics _____

_____

bias _____

_____

Academic Vocabulary *Use a dictionary to define* objective *as an adjective.*

objective _____

_____

Section 2 Scientific Enterprise (continued)

Main Idea	Details

Main Idea

A Work in Progress

I found this information on page _____.

Summarize *how the manner in which people observe natural phenomena has changed over time.*

_____

_____

_____

The History of Meteorology

I found this information on page _____.

Organize *types of weather information that can be measured. Complete the graphic organizer below.*

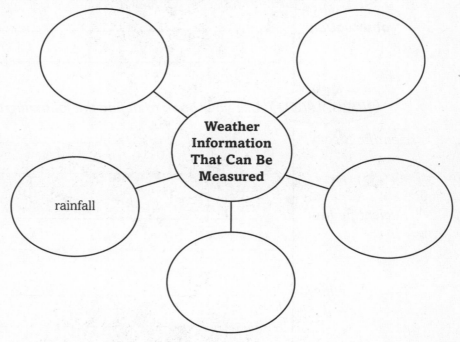

Continuing Research

I found this information on page _____.

Distinguish *between a* scientific theory *and a* scientific law.

_____

_____

_____

_____

_____

_____

Name _____ Date _____

Section 2 Scientific Enterprise (continued)

Main Idea	Details

Limits of Science

I found this information on page _____.

Complete *the following paragraph by filling in the missing terms from the word bank.*

- bad
- ethics
- explain
- good
- limited
- observed
- scientific methods
- tested

Science is _____ by what it can _____.

For a question or problem to be studied through _____,

there must be variables that can be _____, measured,

and _____. Questions that deal with _____

or belief systems cannot be answered by science. Ethics is a system

of understanding what is _____ or _____.

Doing Science Right

I found this information on page _____.

Contrast ethical behavior *in science with* scientific fraud. *Create a table that lists three specific behaviors that are examples of each type of behavior.*

Ethical Behavior	Scientific Fraud

SYNTHESIZE IT

Describe how fraud in scientific research could affect other scientists who research in ethical ways.

_____

_____

_____

The Nature of Science Chapter Wrap-Up

Now that you have read the chapter, think about what you have learned and complete the table below. Compare your previous answers with these.

   1. Write an **A** if you agree with the statement.

   2. Write a **D** if you disagree with the statement.

The Nature of Science	After You Read
• An important part of science is testing, or experimenting.	
• Technology is useful only in the situation for which it was designed.	
• People began studying weather in the 1800s.	
• Science can answer all of the questions that can be asked.	

Review

Use this checklist to help you study.

☐ Review the information you included in your Foldable.

☐ Study your *Science Notebook* on this chapter.

☐ Study the definitions of vocabulary words.

☐ Review daily homework assignments.

☐ Re-read the chapter and review the charts, graphs, and illustrations.

☐ Review the Self Check at the end of each section.

☐ Look over the Chapter Review at the end of the chapter.

SUMMARIZE IT
After reading this chapter, identify three things that you have learned about the nature of science.

_____

_____

_____

_____

Name _____ **Date** _____

Matter

Before You Read

Before you read the chapter, respond to these statements.

    1. Write an **A** if you agree with the statement.

    2. Write a **D** if you disagree with the statement.

Before You Read	Matter
	• When different kinds of atoms combine, they form matter with properties that are different from those of the original atoms.
	• There are about 900 naturally occurring elements on Earth.
	• An atom is stable when it has six electrons in its outer energy level.
	• An object that is less dense than water will float in water.

Construct the Foldable as directed at the beginning of this chapter.

Science Journal

What is matter made of, and how can it take such varied forms? Write what you know now, and compare it with what you learn after you read the chapter.

_____

_____

_____

_____

_____

_____

Matter

Section 1 Atoms

Scan *the headings in Section 1 of your book. Identify three topics that will be discussed.*

1. _____

2. _____

3. _____

Review Vocabulary

Define mass *using your book or a dictionary.*

mass | _____

New Vocabulary

Use your book or a dictionary to explain the differences between the vocabulary terms in each set.

matter
atom
element

_____

_____

_____

_____

proton
neutron
electron

_____

_____

_____

_____

atomic number
mass number
isotope

_____

_____

_____

_____

Academic Vocabulary

Use a dictionary to define sum *to show its meaning in science and math.*

sum | _____

Section 1 **Atoms** (continued)

Main Idea   ## Details

The Building Blocks of Matter

I found this information on page _____.

I found this information on page _____.

Identify *the 2 characteristics that determine the* properties of matter. *List them below.*

1. _____

2. _____

Complete *the graphic organizer below to identify two* characteristics of elements *that make elements different from other kinds of matter.*

Characteristics of Elements

Modeling the Atom

I found this information on page _____.

Define *the 3 basic particles of an atom in the chart below.*

Basic Particles of an Atom		
Name of Particle	Description	Location

Section 1 Atoms (continued)

<table>
<tr><td>

Main Idea

I found this information on page _____ .

</td><td>

Details

Model *the current atomic model of the atom.*

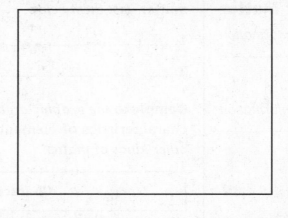

</td></tr>
<tr><td>

Counting Atomic Particles

I found this information on page _____ .

</td><td>

Create *models to illustrate an atom or ion with each of the following:* no charge or neutral; a positive charge; *and* a negative charge. *Be sure to label the particles that make up each atom.*

Neutral

Positive

Negative

</td></tr>
</table>

CONNECT IT Use a periodic table to find the element that has the atomic number 80. Identify the element, the number of protons the element has, and indicate whether the element is a metal, a nonmetal, or a metalloid.

_____

Name _____ Date _____

Matter
Section 2 Combinations of Atoms

Skim *Section 2 of your book. Write three questions that come to mind. Look for answers to your questions as you read the section.*

1. _____

2. _____

3. _____

Review Vocabulary

Define force *using your book or a dictionary.*

force

_____

New Vocabulary

Read each definition. Use your book to write the correct vocabulary term on the line next to each definition.

_____ negatively or positively charged atom

_____ composed of two or more substances that are not chemically combined

_____ a mixture that is evenly mixed throughout, also known as a homogeneous mixture

_____ atoms of more than one type of element that are chemically bonded together

_____ group of atoms held together by covalent bonds

_____ mixture that is evenly mixed throughout

_____ mixture that is not mixed evenly and each component retains its own properties

Academic Vocabulary

Use a dictionary to define formula *to show its scientific meaning.*

formula

_____

_____

Section 2 Combinations of Atoms (continued)

⟨Main Idea⟩ _____ **⟨Details⟩** _____

Interactions of Atoms

I found this information on page _____.

Organize *information about the* interactions of atoms *by completing the outline below.*

   I. Interactions of Atoms

      A. Compounds

         1. _____

             _____

         2. _____

             _____

         3. _____

             _____

      B. Chemical Properties

         1. _____

             _____

         2. _____

             _____

Bonding

I found this information on page _____.

Predict *how an atom with an unstable outer energy level will likely form a chemical bond with another atom.*

_____

_____

_____

I found this information on page _____.

Complete *the graphic organizer below to identify the types of* chemical bonds that form compounds.

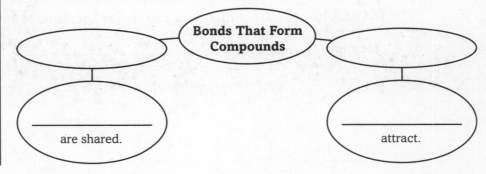

Bonds That Form Compounds

are shared.

attract.

Section 2 Combinations of Atoms (continued)

Main Idea | Details

I found this information on page _____.

Compare metallic bonds *and* hydrogen bonds *by completing the chart below.*

Type of Bond	Description	Unique Characteristic
Metallic Bond		
Hydrogen Bond		

Mixtures

I found this information on page _____.

Create *a graphic organizer to identify and define the* two types of mixtures.

```
            ┌─────────────────────┐
            │  Types of Mixtures  │
            └──┬───────────────┬──┘
```

Separating Mixtures and Compounds

I found this information on page _____.

Summarize *how* mixtures *and* compounds *can be separated.*

Mixture: _____

Compound: _____

EVALUATE IT

A kitchen contains the following: lemonade, snack mix, mixed seasonings, vinegar, olives in water, and carbonated water. Classify each of these as a homogeneous mixture or a heterogeneous mixture.

_____

_____

Matter

Section 3 Properties of Matter

Scan *the* What You'll Learn *statements in Section 3 of your book. Identify three topics that will be discussed in this section.*

1. _____

2. _____

3. _____

Review Vocabulary

Define energy *using your book or a dictionary.*

energy _____

_____

New Vocabulary

Use your book to define density. *Then use the term in a sentence to show its scientific meaning.*

density _____

_____

_____

_____

Academic Vocabulary

Use a dictionary to define volume *to show its scientific meaning. Then write a sentence that includes the word.*

volume _____

_____

_____

_____

Section 3 Properties of Matter (continued)

Main Idea

Details

Physical Properties of Matter

I found this information on page _____.

Define physical property. *Then write five examples of physical properties.*

Definition: _____

_____

Examples: _____

States of Matter

I found this information on page _____.

Classify *the different* states of matter *by completing the graphic organizer below.*

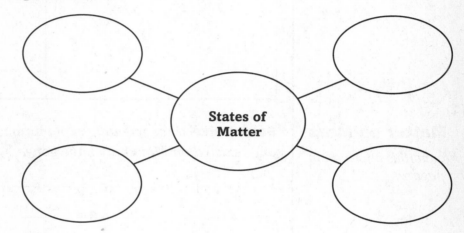

States of Matter

Changing the State of Matter

I found this information on page _____.

Predict *how each of the following conditions would affect the state of matter.*

Liquid matter reaches its freezing point: _____

_____

Liquid matter reaches its boiling point: _____

_____

Pressure on liquid matter near its boiling point is decreased:

_____

_____

Section 3 Properties of Matter (continued)

Main Idea

Changes in Physical Properties

I found this information on page _____.

Matter on Mars

I found this information on page _____.

Details

Contrast *the way that the* density *of water changes when it freezes with the way the density of most other materials changes when those materials turn solid.*

Contrasting Density of Substances	
Water	Most other materials

Summarize *three scientific explanations of where the water that once existed on Mars may have gone.*

1. _____

_____

2. _____

_____

3. _____

_____

SYNTHESIZE IT

Predict whether a copper penny would float or sink when dropped into a pan of melted copper. Support your reasoning with information from this section.

_____

_____

_____

Tie It Together

What's the matter?

Analyze the two samples of matter below by answering the following questions:

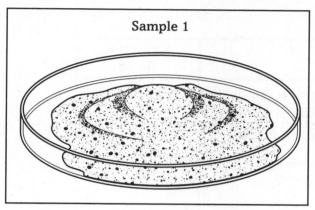

Sample 1

Iron and sulfur

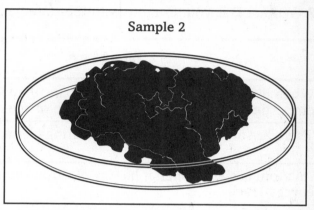

Sample 2

Iron and sulfur after being heated

1. What are the physical properties of each sample?

Sample 1: _____

Sample 2: _____

2. Identify each substance as either a mixture or a compound. Explain your reasoning.

Sample 1: _____

_____

Sample 2: _____

_____

3. Predict whether the matter that makes up each sample could be separated physically, chemically, or not at all. Support your reasoning.

Sample 1: _____

_____

_____

Sample 2: _____

_____

Matter   Chapter Wrap-Up

Now that you have read the chapter, think about what you have learned and complete the table below. Compare your previous answers with these.

1. Write an **A** if you agree with the statement.
2. Write a **D** if you disagree with the statement.

Matter	After You Read
• When different kinds of atoms combine, they form matter with properties that are different from those of the original atoms.	
• There are about 900 naturally occurring elements on Earth.	
• An atom is stable when it has six electrons in its outer energy level.	
• An object that is less dense than water will float in water.	

Review

Use this checklist to help you study.

☐ Review the information you included in your Foldable.

☐ Study your *Science Notebook* on this chapter.

☐ Study the definitions of vocabulary words.

☐ Review daily homework assignments.

☐ Re-read the chapter and review the charts, graphs, and illustrations.

☐ Review the Self Check at the end of each section.

☐ Look over the Chapter Review at the end of the chapter.

SUMMARIZE IT After reading this chapter, summarize three main ideas from the chapter.

_____

_____

_____

_____

Minerals

Before You Read

Before you read the chapter, respond to these statements.

1. Write an **A** if you agree with the statement.
2. Write a **D** if you disagree with the statement.

Before You Read	Minerals
	• Atoms in a mineral are arranged in an orderly pattern.
	• Minerals are made in the lab from natural materials.
	• Diamonds are so hard they cannot be broken.
	• Minerals are a source of metals and other useful elements.

Construct the Foldable as directed at the beginning of this chapter.

Science Journal

Write two questions that you would ask a gemologist—one who studies gems and gemstones—about the minerals that he or she works with.

_____

_____

_____

_____

_____

_____

_____

_____

Minerals
Section 1 Minerals

Skim *through Section 1 of your book. Read the headings and examine the illustrations. Write three questions that come to mind.*

1. _____

2. _____

3. _____

Review Vocabulary

Define atoms *using your book or a dictionary.*

atoms

_____

_____

New Vocabulary

Use your book to define the following terms.

mineral

_____

_____

crystal

_____

_____

magma

_____

_____

silicate

_____

_____

Academic Vocabulary

Use a dictionary to define occur.

occur

_____

_____

Section 1 Minerals (continued)

<table>
<tr><td>**Main Idea**</td><td>**Details**</td></tr>
</table>

What is a mineral?

I found this information on page _____.

Organize *the four characteristics shared by all* minerals *in the concept web below.*

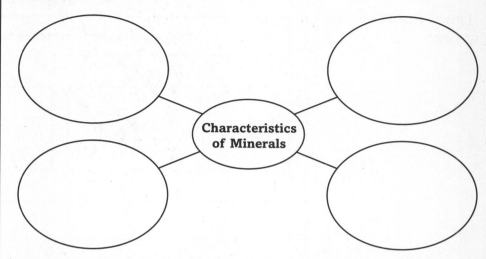

The Structure of Minerals

I found this information on page _____.

Model *the structure of minerals by using simple geometric shapes or dot patterns to represent atoms arranged in a* crystalline pattern.

Summarize *how* atoms *are arranged in* minerals.

_____

_____

_____

Section 1 Minerals (continued)

Main Idea	Details

The Structure of Minerals

I found this information on page _____.

Sequence *the two processes by which minerals form from solution by completing the diagram below.*

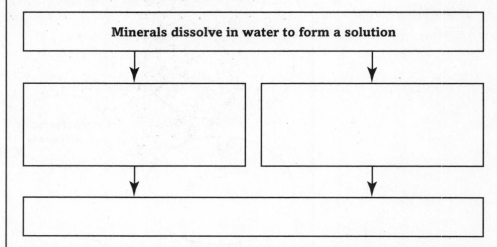

Minerals dissolve in water to form a solution

Mineral Compositions and Groups

I found this information on page _____.

Analyze *the chart of* Elements in Earth's Crust *that is provided in your book, and complete the following sentences.*

1. Most of Earth's crust is made up of only _____ elements.

2. _____ and _____ are the most abundant elements, making up about _____ percent of Earth's crust.

3. Six other common elements are _____

_____.

Distinguish *between a* carbonate *and a* silicate. *Then identify two carbonates and two silicates.*

_____

_____

_____

CONNECT IT

Critique the statement "Coal is an essential mineral for society."

_____

_____

_____

Minerals
Section 2 Mineral Identification

Predict *three things that you expect to learn based on the headings in Section 2.*

1. _____

   _____

2. _____

   _____

3. _____

   _____

Review Vocabulary
Define physical property *using your book or a dictionary.*

physical property   _____

_____

New Vocabulary
Write the correct vocabulary term next to its definition.

_____   measure of how easily a mineral can be scratched

_____   describes the way a mineral reflects light from its surface; can be metallic or nonmetallic

_____   color of a mineral when it is in powdered form

_____   physical property of some minerals that causes them to break along smooth, flat surfaces

_____   physical property of some minerals that causes them to break with uneven, rough, or jagged surfaces

Academic Vocabulary
Use a dictionary to define obvious.

obvious   _____

_____

Section 2 Mineral Identification (continued)

◀ **Main Idea** ▶ _____ ◀ **Details** ▶ _____

Physical Properties

I found this information on page _____ .

Summarize *why attempting to identify a mineral by its color alone may sometimes be deceiving.*

_____

_____

_____

I found this information on page _____ .

Compare and contrast mineral hardness *with the hardness of common objects by completing the diagram below.*

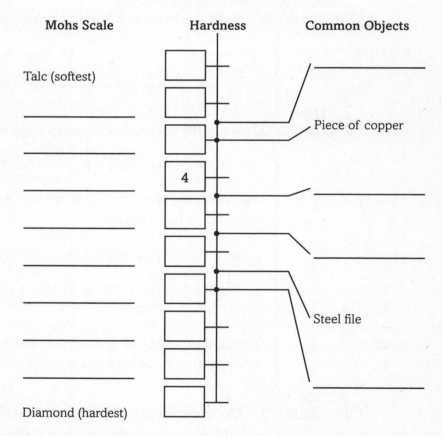

Mineral Hardness

Mohs Scale — Hardness — Common Objects

Talc (softest)

_____

_____

_____

4

_____

_____

_____

_____

_____

Diamond (hardest)

Piece of copper

Steel file

Analyze *the chart by completing the prompts.*

Your fingernail can scratch the minerals _____ and _____ .

A streak plate is softer than the minerals _____, _____,

and _____ .

Section 2 Mineral Identification (continued)

Main Idea	Details

Physical Properties

I found this information on page _____.

Create *a concept web that identifies* six properties *used to identify minerals.*

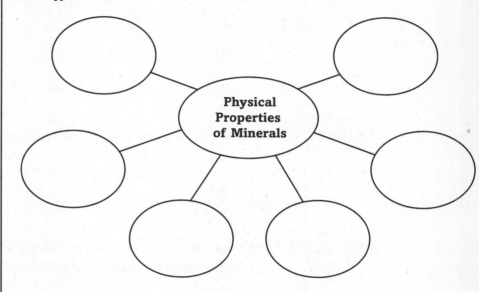

I found this information on page _____.

Identify *the unique properties of* **lodestone** *and* calcite.

lodestone	calcite

CONNECT IT Suppose you were given an assignment to scratch your name into a piece of glass on a special name plate. Identify which of the following minerals you could use. Which would work best? Support your choices with reasons and examples.

diamond   gypsum   apatite   quartz

_____

_____

_____

_____

Minerals
Section 3 Uses of Minerals

Predict *three things that might be discussed in Section 3. Read the headings to help you make your predictions.*

1. _____

2. _____

3. _____

Review Vocabulary

Define metal *using your book or a dictionary.*

metal

_____

_____

New Vocabulary

Use your book to define the following terms. Then use each term in a sentence that shows its scientific meaning.

gem

_____

_____

_____

_____

ore

_____

_____

_____

_____

Academic Vocabulary

Use a dictionary to define accurate.

accurate

_____

_____

Section 3 Uses of Minerals

Main Idea / Details

Gems

I found this information on page _____.

Summarize *what distinguishes* gems *from common samples of minerals.*

_____

_____

I found this information on page _____.

Complete *the chart to list some gems and their uses.*

Useful Gems	
Gem	Uses
	in cutting tools
Rubies	
Quartz crystals	

Useful Elements in Minerals

I found this information on page _____.

Sequence *the stages from ore, to refined element, to manufactured product.*

Ore	Element	Product
	iron	frying pans, nails
Bauxite		
	zinc	
Ilmenite or rutile		

Section 3 Uses of Minerals

Main Idea

Useful Elements in Minerals

I found this information on page _____.

Details

Complete *the flow chart to describe how vein minerals form.*

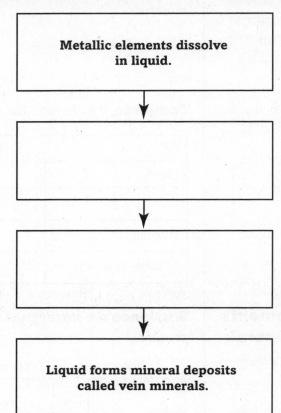

Metallic elements dissolve
in liquid.

Liquid forms mineral deposits
called vein minerals.

SYNTHESIZE IT

Infer why aluminum is more expensive than iron or steel.
Compare the availability of aluminum recycling to that of iron or steel. Explain
your reasoning.

_____

_____

_____

_____

_____

_____

Tie It Together

Synthesize

Create a concept web to summarize what you have learned about mineral characteristics, composition, identifcation, and uses. (Hint: You may find it easier to write a list of facts to include, and then organize them into the web.)

_____
_____
_____
_____
_____
_____
_____
_____
_____
_____

Minerals Chapter Wrap-Up

Now that you have read the chapter, think about what you have learned and complete the table below. Compare your previous answers with these.

1. Write an **A** if you agree with the statement.
2. Write a **D** if you disagree with the statement.

Minerals	After You Read
• Atoms in a mineral are arranged in an orderly pattern.	
• Minerals are made in the lab from natural materials.	
• Diamonds are so hard they cannot be broken.	
• Minerals are a source of metals and other useful elements.	

Review

Use this checklist to help you study.

☐ Review the information you included in your Foldable.

☐ Study your *Science Notebook* on this chapter.

☐ Study the definitions of vocabulary words.

☐ Review daily homework assignments.

☐ Re-read the chapter and review the charts, graphs, and illustrations.

☐ Review the Self Check at the end of each section.

☐ Look over the Chapter Review at the end of the chapter.

SUMMARIZE IT After reading this chapter, identify three things that you have learned about minerals.

_____

_____

_____

_____

Rocks

Before You Read

Before you read the chapter, respond to these statements.

   1. Write an **A** if you agree with the statement.

   2. Write a **D** if you disagree with the statement.

Before You Read	Rocks
	• Heat can melt rock.
	• Rocks from lava form only under Earth's surface.
	• Rocks on Earth change slowly over time.
	• Many rocks form in layers.

 *Construct the Foldable as directed at the beginning of this chapter.*

Science Journal

Are you a rock collector? If so, write two sentences about your favorite rock. If not, describe rocks that you have seen in enough detail that a non-sighted person could visualize them.

_____

_____

_____

_____

_____

_____

Rocks
Section 1 The Rock Cycle

Skim *Section 1 of your book. Read the headings and examine the illustrations. Write three questions that come to mind.*

1. _____

_____

2. _____

_____

3. _____

_____

Review Vocabulary **Define** mineral *using your book or a dictionary.*

mineral _____

_____

New Vocabulary *Use your book to define the following terms. Then use each term in an original sentence to show its scientific meaning.*

rock _____

_____

_____

_____

rock cycle _____

_____

_____

_____

Academic Vocabulary *Use your book or a dictionary to define erode.*

erode _____

_____

Section 1 The Rock Cycle (continued)

Main Idea	Details

What is a rock?

I found this information on page _____.

Complete *the blanks in this description of* rock.

Most common rock contains one or more _____

such as _____ or _____.

Rock types may also contain _____,

_____, or _____.

The Rock Cycle

I found this information on page _____.

Classify *the three major types of rocks. Complete the graphic organizer.*

Types of Rocks

I found this information on page _____.

Model *the rock cycle.* **Draw a diagram showing the ways in which rock can change. Include the five types of rock and the processes through which they can change.**

Section 1 The Rock Cycle (continued)

<table>
<tr><td>~Main Idea~</td><td>_____ ~Details~ _____</td></tr>
</table>

The Rock Cycle

I found this information on page _____ .

Organize *ways that each form of rock can change in the rock cycle. Complete the flowcharts.*

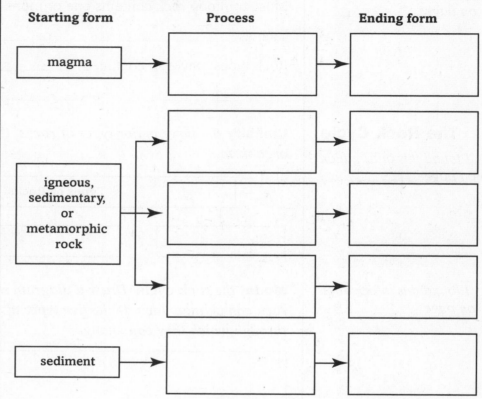

Starting form   Process   Ending form

magma

igneous,
sedimentary,
or
metamorphic
rock

sediment

I found this information on page _____ .

Complete *the blanks in the statements about the rock cycle.*

In the rock cycle, matter is _____ lost or destroyed. It is

_____ and used in other forms. Neither _____ ,

weathering, nor _____ destroys matter.

SUMMARIZE IT

Choose a form of rock. Then use the rock cycle diagram to describe all the possible ways that rock could form.

_____

_____

_____

_____

Rocks
Section 2 Igneous Rocks

Scan *the headings of Section 2. Identify three categories of formation of igneous rocks and three classification groups.*

1. _____ , _____ , or _____

2. _____ , _____ , or _____

Review Vocabulary

Explain how an element *is different from a* compound *or* a *mixture.*

element

_____

_____

_____

New Vocabulary

Use your book to define the following terms.

igneous rock

_____

_____

lava

_____

_____

intrusive

_____

_____

extrusive

_____

_____

Academic Vocabulary

Use your book or a dictionary to define infer. *Then explain why inferring is important to scientists.*

infer

_____

_____

_____

Section 2 Igneous Rocks (continued)

Main Idea

Formation of Igneous Rocks

I found this information on page _____.

Details

Complete *the flow chart about* lava.

```
┌──────────────────┐        ┌──────────────────┐
│                  │        │                  │
└──────────────────┘        └──────────────────┘
         │                           ↑
      melts                      At the
      to form                    surface
         │                   it becomes
         ↓                           
┌────────────────────────────────────────────────┐
│                                                 │
│ _____  which rises because it is _____ │
│                                                 │
│ _____ .  │
└────────────────────────────────────────────────┘
```

I found this information on page _____.

Identify *two sources of heat that melt rocks beneath Earth's surface.*

1. _____

2. _____

I found this information on page _____.

Distinguish *among the types of* igneous rocks *and the processes by which they form. Complete the chart.*

Type of Rock	Characteristics	Formation Process
Intrusive		
Extrusive		
Volcanic Glass		

Section 2 Igneous Rocks (continued)

Main Idea	Details

Classifying Igneous Rocks

I found this information on page _____ .

Sequence *the three types of igneous rock. The arrows show how the density, silica content, and iron and magnesium content increase among the types of igneous rock.*

Density $\longleftarrow$

Silica $\longrightarrow$

Iron and Magnesium $\longleftarrow$

I found this information on page _____ .

Analyze *how the characteristics of each type of magma affect how it rises to the surface.*

Type of Magma	Characteristics	How It Rises to the Surface
Basaltic		oozes out through cracks in ocean floor or spills out of volcanos
Granitic		
Andesitic		

SYNTHESIZE IT Classify the following rocks on the basis of what you have learned from this section. Identify whether each is intrusive or extrusive, and identify its composition as basaltic, granitic, or andesitic.

a) a dark-colored rock containing a high level of iron that formed from magma that cooled beneath Earth's surface

b) a light-colored rock with high silica content that formed from lava on Earth's surface

Rocks
Section 3 Metamorphic Rocks

Scan *the headings in Section 3. Predict two subjects that you expect will be discussed in this section.*

1. _____

_____

2. _____

_____

Review Vocabulary

Define pressure *using your book or a dictionary. Then write a sentence that shows its scientific meaning.*

pressure   _____

_____

_____

New Vocabulary

Write the vocabulary term that matches each definition.

_____ rock formed when heat, pressure, or fluids act on other rock to change its form, its composition, or both

_____ describes metamorphic rock whose mineral grains line up in parallel layers

_____ describes metamorphic rock whose mineral grains generally do not form layers

Academic Vocabulary

Use a dictionary to define transform.

transform   _____

_____

Section 3 **Metamorphic Rocks** (continued)

⬤ ◖ **Main Idea** ◗ _____ ◖ **Details** ◗ _____

Formation of Metamorphic Rocks

I found this information on page _____.

Organize *information about the processes that can form* metamorphic rock.

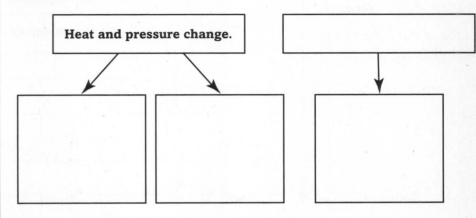

Heat and pressure change.

I found this information on page _____.

Sequence *the types of rocks in the process from shale to gneiss.*

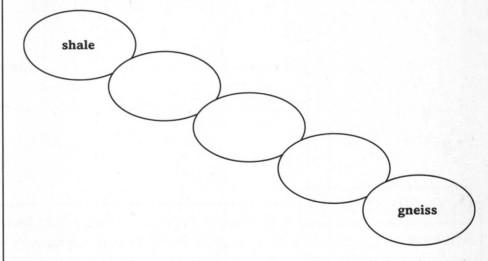

shale

gneiss

I found this information on page _____.

Describe *the formation of* foliated *rock.*

_____

_____

Describe *the growth of grains in sandstone to change it to* quartzite, *a* nonfoliated *rock.*

_____

_____

Section 3 Metamorphic Rocks (continued)

Main Idea

Classifying Metamorphic Rocks

I found this information on page _____.

Details

Summarize *the two textures of metamorphic rocks. Describe each texture and give two examples of rocks with that texture.*

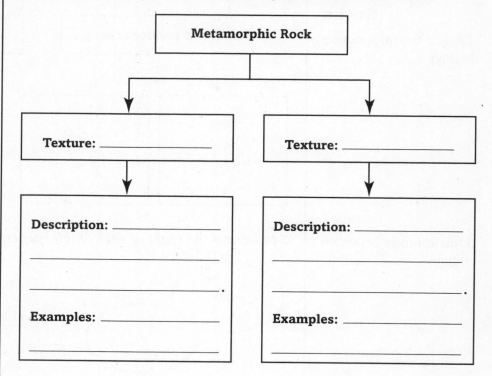

```
                    Metamorphic Rock

    Texture: _____        Texture: _____

    Description: _____    Description: _____
    _____        _____
    _____.       _____.

    Examples: _____      Examples: _____
    _____        _____
```

SYNTHESIZE IT   A planner is designing a new office building. The building will have an open courtyard around it. Analyze what metamorphic rocks the planner might use. Explain why each rock would be useful.

_____

_____

_____

_____

_____

_____

Rocks
Section 4 Sedimentary Rocks

Skim *Section 4. Write three questions you would like to answer. Find the answers to your questions as you read.*

1. _____
   _____

2. _____
   _____

3. _____
   _____

Review Vocabulary

Define weathering *using your book or a dictionary.*

weathering

_____
_____

New Vocabulary

Write a sentence from Section 4 that uses each term.

sediments

_____
_____

sedimentary rock

_____
_____

compaction

_____
_____

cementation

_____
_____

Academic Vocabulary

Use a dictionary to define consist.

consist

_____
_____

Section 4 Sedimentary Rocks (continued)

Main Idea — Details

Formation of Sedimentary Rocks

I found this information on page _____.

Model *the relative ages of sedimentary rock layers. Draw a cross-section of undisturbed sedimentary rocks. Label the oldest and youngest layers.*

Classifying Sedimentary Rocks

I found this information on page _____.

Identify and define *the three types of sedimentary rock in the graphic organizer below.*

Sedimentary Rocks

Detrital Sedimentary Rocks

I found this information on page _____.

Classify *types of detrital sedimentary rock by the size and shape (where shape is relevant) of the particles found in them.*

Type	Conglomerate	Breccia	Sandstone	Shale
Size/ shape				
Sketch of rock				

Section 4 Sedimentary Rocks (continued)

Main Idea	Details

Chemical Sedimentary Rocks

I found this information on page _____ .

Sequence *the steps in the formation of chemical sedimentary rocks. Complete the graphic organizer.*

> **1.** Minerals are dissolved in water.

> **2.**

> **3.**

> **4.**

Organic Sedimentary Rocks

I found this information on page _____ .

Identify *two examples of chemical sedimentary rocks.*

Examples: _____ _____

List *three organic sedimentary rocks and explain how each forms.*

Rock: _____

How It Forms: _____

_____

Rock: _____

How It Forms: _____

_____

Rock: _____

How It Forms: _____

_____

CONNECT IT Describe at least four uses for sedimentary rocks in your life.

_____

_____

_____

ROCKS Chapter Wrap-Up

Now that you have read the chapter, think about what you have learned and complete the table below. Compare your previous answers with these.

1. Write an **A** if you agree with the statement.
2. Write a **D** if you disagree with the statement.

Rocks	After You Read
• Heat can melt rock.	
• Rocks from lava form only under Earth's surface.	
• Rocks on Earth change slowly over time.	
• Many rocks form in layers.	

Review

Use this checklist to help you study.

☐ Review the information you included in your Foldable.

☐ Study your *Science Notebook* on this chapter.

☐ Study the definitions of vocabulary words.

☐ Review daily homework assignments.

☐ Re-read the chapter and review the charts, graphs, and illustrations.

☐ Review the Self Check at the end of each section.

☐ Look over the Chapter Review at the end of the chapter.

SYNTHESIZE IT

The rock cycle is said to have no beginning and no end. Discuss why this is true. Use an example to illustrate your answer.

_____

_____

_____

_____

_____

Earth's Energy and Mineral Resources

Before You Read

Preview the chapter including section titles and the section headings. Complete the chart by listing at least one idea for each of the three sections in each column.

K What I know	W What I want to find out

FOLDABLES™
Study Organizer

Construct the Foldable as directed at the beginning of this chapter.

Science Journal

Write three ways electricity may be generated at a power plant.

_____

_____

_____

_____

_____

_____

Earth's Energy and Mineral Resources

Section 1 Nonrenewable Energy Resources

Scan *Section 1 of your book, using the checklist below.*

☐ Read all section titles.

☐ Read all boldface words.

☐ Look at all of the pictures.

☐ Think about what you already know about nonrenewable resources.

Write three facts that you discovered about nonrenewable resources as you scanned this section.

1. _____

2. _____

3. _____

Review Vocabulary   **Define** fuel.

fuel _____

New Vocabulary   *Use your book or a dictionary to define the vocabulary terms.*

resource _____

_____

nonrenewable resource _____

_____

conservation _____

Academic Vocabulary   *Use a dictionary to define* extract.

extract _____

Section 1 Nonrenewable Energy Resources (continued)

Main Idea
Details

Energy

I found this information on page _____.

Complete *the paragraph below to describe* resources *and* energy.

A _____ is any material used to satisfy a need. Most

energy resources used to generate electricity are _____.

Nonrenewable resources are _____

_____.

Fossil Fuels

I found this information on page _____.

Organize *information about* fossil fuels *by completing the outline.*

  I. Fossil Fuels

    A. Made of _____

    B. Formed over _____ of years

    C. Include:

      1. _____

      2. _____

      3. _____

    D. Used to:

      1. Make gasoline for _____

      2. Heat _____

      3. Generate _____

I found this information on page _____.

Complete *the chart describing the stages of* coal formation. *Then identify the change in the amount of energy contained in the fuel.*

Formation of Coal

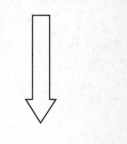

1. | peat | contains _____ energy

2. | _____ |

3. | _____ |

4. | _____ | contains _____ energy

Section 1 Nonrenewable Energy Resources (continued)

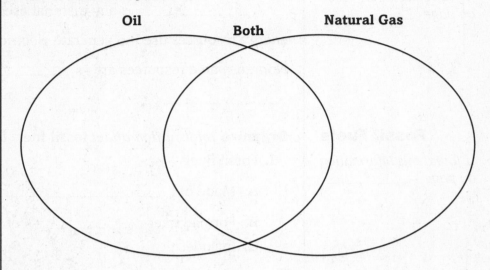

Main Idea

Details

Fossil Fuels

I found this information on page _____.

Compare oil *and* natural gas *by completing the Venn diagram with at least nine facts.*

Oil   Both   Natural Gas

Removing Fossil Fuels from the Ground and Fossil Fuel Reserves

I found this information on page _____.

Create *a graphic organizer to identify the ways fossil fuels are removed from the ground. Then complete the sentence below.*

Fossil fuel _____ are the useable and cost-effective part

of existing fossil fuel _____.

Energy from Atoms

I found this information on page _____.

Sequence *the steps in a* nuclear chain reaction.

_____ are fired at fuel rods containing _____.	Neutrons hit _____ atoms. The atoms split apart, releasing _____ and _____.	More _____ atoms split, releasing more _____ and more _____.

Earth's Energy and Mineral Resources

Section 2 Renewable Energy Resources

Predict *three things that might be discussed in Section 2 as you read the headings.*

1. _____

_____

2. _____

_____

3. _____

_____

Review Vocabulary

Define *the scientific term* energy *using your book or a dictionary.*

energy _____

New Vocabulary

Use your book or a dictionary to define the vocabulary terms.

renewable resource _____

_____

geothermal energy _____

_____

biomass energy _____

_____

Academic Vocabulary

Use a dictionary to define derive.

derive _____

Section 2 Renewable Energy Resources (continued)

Main Idea	Details

Renewable Energy Resources

I found this information on page _____.

Contrast passive *and* active solar energy *by providing examples.*

An example of passive solar energy is _____

_____ .

An example of active solar energy is _____

_____ .

I found this information on page _____.

Compare *the advantages and disadvantages of generating electricity from* wind energy.

Wind Energy as Source of Electricity	
Advantages	Disadvantages

I found this information on page _____.

Model *a* hydroelectric power plant. *Use the figure in your book.*

Section 2 Renewable Energy Resources (continued)

Main Idea	Details

Renewable Energy Resources

I found this information on page _____.

Identify *three problems associated with* geothermal power.

1. _____

_____

2. _____

_____

3. _____

_____

Other Renewable Energy Resources

I found this information on page _____.

Compare *these examples of* biomass *that can be used to generate energy. List the advantages and disadvantages of each.*

Biomass Energy		
Material	**Advantages**	**Disadvantages**
Wood		
Alcohol		
Garbage		

Earth's Energy and Mineral Resources

Section 3 Mineral Resources

Skim *through Section 3 of your book. Read the headings and look at the illustrations. Write three questions that come to mind.*

1. _____

2. _____

3. _____

Review Vocabulary

Define metal *using your book or a dictionary.*

metal _____

_____

New Vocabulary

Use your book or a dictionary to define the vocabulary terms.

mineral resources _____

_____

ore _____

_____

recycling _____

Academic Vocabulary

Use a dictionary to define obtain.

obtain _____

_____

Section 3 Mineral Resources (continued)

Main Idea

Metallic Mineral Resources

I found this information on page _____.

I found this information on page _____.

Details

List *the three things that are required for a mineral deposit to be considered an* ore.

A mineral deposit is considered an ore when:
1.
2.
3.

Sequence *the steps in separating a useful mineral from its ore by completing the graphic organizer below. Then define* smelting.

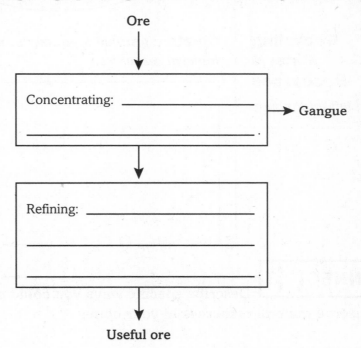

Ore

Concentrating: _____

_____ .

→ Gangue

Refining: _____

_____

_____ .

Useful ore

Smelting: _____

_____

Section 3 Mineral Resources (continued)

Main Idea　　　　　　　　　**Details**

Nonmetallic Mineral Resources

I found this information on page _____.

Classify mineral resources *and* building materials *by completing the Venn diagram with at least seven materials.*

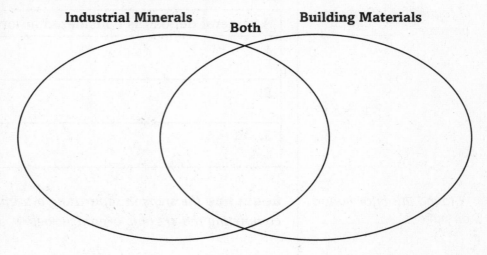

Industrial Minerals　　　Both　　　Building Materials

Recycling Mineral Resources

I found this information on page _____.

Create *a graphic organizer to identify three ways to conserve mineral resources.*

CONNECT IT　Describe specific ways you could practice each of the three ways to conserve mineral resources in your home.

_____

_____

_____

_____

_____

Tie It Together

Evaluate Energy Resources

Identify which alternative energy resource you think could best serve your community. Write a report explaining why you believe it would be the best choice. Discuss advantages and disadvantages for your community of using the alternative energy resource.

_____

_____

_____

_____

_____

_____

_____

_____

_____

_____

_____

_____

_____

_____

_____

_____

_____

_____

_____

_____

_____

Earth's Energy and Mineral Resources   Chapter Wrap-Up

Review the ideas you listed in the chart at the beginning of the chapter. Cross out any incorrect information in the first column. Then complete the chart by filling in the third column.

K What I know	W What I want to find out	L What I learned

Review

Use this checklist to help you study.

☐ Review the information you included in your Foldable.

☐ Study your *Science Notebook* on this chapter.

☐ Study the definitions of vocabulary words.

☐ Review daily homework assignments.

☐ Re-read the chapter and review the charts, graphs, and illustrations.

☐ Review the Self Check at the end of each section.

☐ Look over the Chapter Review at the end of the chapter.

SUMMARIZE IT
After reading this chapter, identify three things that you have learned about Earth's energy and mineral resources.

_____

_____

_____

_____

Views of Earth

Before You Read

Before you read the chapter, respond to these statements.

1. Write an **A** if you agree with the statement.
2. Write a **D** if you disagree with the statement.

Before You Read	Views of Earth
	• All mountains form in the same way.
	• Lines of longitude run parallel to the equator.
	• All maps of Earth distort the shapes and sizes of landmasses.

 *Construct the Foldable as directed at the beginning of this chapter.*

Science Journal

Assume that you want to build a home and have a satellite photo to guide you. Describe where you would build your new home and why you would build at your chosen location.

_____

_____

_____

_____

_____

_____

_____

Views of Earth
Section 1 Landforms

Skim *the headings in Section 1. Write three questions that come to mind from reading these headings.*

1. _____

2. _____

3. _____

Review Vocabulary

landform

Define landform *to show its scientific meaning.*

_____

_____

New Vocabulary

Write the vocabulary term that matches each definition.

_____ large, flat area, often found in the interior regions of continents

_____ flat, raised area of land made up of nearly horizontal rocks that have been uplifted by forces within Earth

_____ mountain in which rock layers are folded

_____ mountain formed when blocks of Earth's crust are pushed up by forces inside Earth

_____ mountain made of huge, tilted blocks of rock separated from surrounding rock by faults

_____ mountain formed when molten material reaches the surface through a weak area of Earth's crust

Academic Vocabulary

expose

Use a dictionary to define expose.

_____

_____

Name _____ **Date** _____

Section 1 Landforms (continued)

Main Idea | **Details**

Plains

I found this information on page _____ .

Distinguish *two reasons that* plains *are useful for agriculture.*

1. _____

_____

2. _____

_____

I found this information on page _____ .

Compare and contrast *coastal plains and interior plains.*

	Coastal Plains	**Interior Plains**
Location		
Characteristics		

I found this information on page _____ .

Summarize *key characteristics of the Great Plains.*

The Great Plains are an example of a(n) _____ .

They are located _____

_____ . The area is _____

and covered with _____ . The Great Plains

are made of _____ .

Plateaus

I found this information on page _____ .

Compare and contrast *plains and* plateaus. *Complete the Venn diagram with at least three facts.*

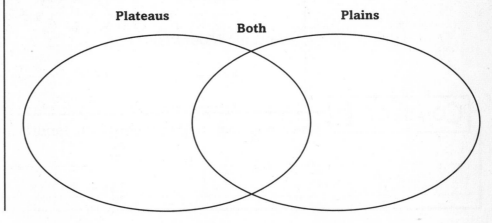

Plateaus — Both — Plains

Section 1 Landforms (continued)

<table>
<tr><td>Main Idea</td><td>Details</td></tr>
</table>

Mountains

I found this information on page _____ .

Model *the four types of* mountains. *Draw a diagram of each type.*

Folded Mountain	Upwarped Mountain

Fault-Block Mountain	Volcanic Mountain

Summarize *how mountains form. Give an example of each.*

Folded Mountain: _____

_____

_____

Upwarped Mountain: _____

_____

_____

Fault-Block Mountain: _____

_____

_____

Volcanic Mountain: _____

_____

_____

CONNECT IT

Use a physical map to identify the landforms in your area.

_____

_____

Views of Earth
Section 2 Viewpoints

Preview *the* What You'll Learn *statements for Section 2. Predict three topics that will be discussed in this section.*

1. _____

2. _____

3. _____

Review Vocabulary **Define** pole *as it is used when describing Earth.*

pole

_____

_____

New Vocabulary *Define each vocabulary term.*

equator

_____

_____

latitude

_____

_____

prime meridian

_____

_____

longitude

_____

_____

Academic Vocabulary *Use a dictionary to define* parallel *as an adjective. Then find a sentence in Section 2 that contains the term.*

parallel

_____

_____

_____

Section 2 Viewpoints (continued)

Main Idea

Latitude and Longitude

I found this information on page _____.

Details

Model *the system used to measure position on Earth.*

- Draw a view of Earth.
- Label important features on the diagram with the following terms.

equator   prime meridian   90°S latitude
north pole   0° latitude   90°N latitude
south pole

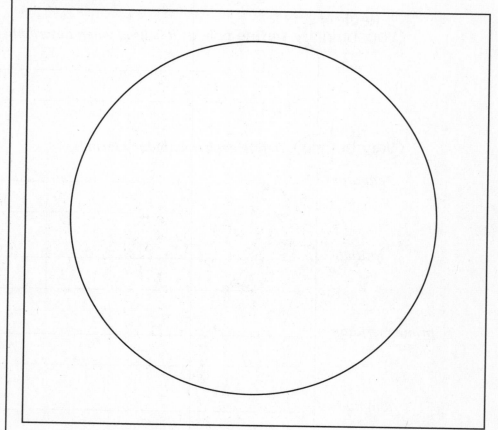

Summarize *how* latitude *and* longitude *are measured.*

Latitude is measured _____

_____ .

Longitude is measured _____

_____ .

Degrees of latitude and longitude are divided into _____

and _____ .

Section 2 Viewpoints (continued)

Main Idea	**Details**

Time Zones

I found this information on page _____.

Organize *information about time zones. Complete the outline.*

Time Zones

  I. Measuring time

    A. _____

    _____

    B. _____

    _____

  II. Characteristics of time zones

    A. _____

    _____

    B. _____

    _____

    C. _____

    _____

Calendar Dates

I found this information on page _____.

Summarize *what a person should do when crossing the International Date Line. Complete the cause-and-effect diagrams.*

| Travel west across the International Date Line | → | |
| Travel east across the International Date Line | → | |

SYNTHESIZE IT Look at the map of time zones in your book. Infer why the International Date Line does not follow the 180° meridian exactly.

_____

_____

_____

Views of Earth
Section 3 Maps

Scan *the section headings, bold words, and illustrations. Write two facts that you discovered as you scanned the section.*

1. _____

2. _____

Review Vocabulary **Define** globe *to show its scientific meaning.*

globe | _____

New Vocabulary *Use your book to define each vocabulary term.*

conic projection | _____

_____

topographic map | _____

_____

contour line | _____

_____

map scale | _____

_____

map legend | _____

_____

Academic Vocabulary *Use a dictionary to define* physical. *Use* physical *in a sentence to show its scientific meaning.*

physical | _____

_____

Section 3 Maps (continued)

Main Idea | Details

Map Projections

I found this information on page _____ .

I found this information on page _____ .

Define map. *Then complete the statements below about map projections.*

A map is _____ .

A map projection is made when _____

_____ .

All map projections _____ the shapes and sizes of land-

masses to some extent.

Compare and contrast Mercator, Robinson, *and* conic projections.

	Mercator	Robinson	Conic
How is it made?			
What does it show accurately?			
How is it used?			

Topographic Maps

I found this information on page _____ .

Summarize *the purpose of a* topographic map.

_____

_____

_____

_____

Section 3 Maps (continued)

Main Idea	Details

I found this information on page _____ .

Organize *information about* contour lines *in the concept web.*

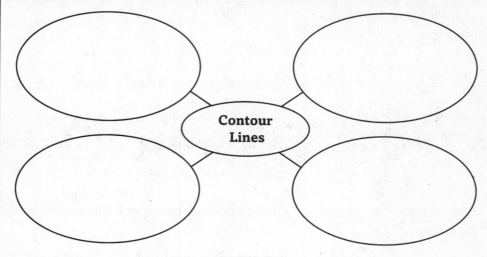

Contour Lines

I found this information on page _____ .

Summarize *what a* map scale *and* map legend *show.*

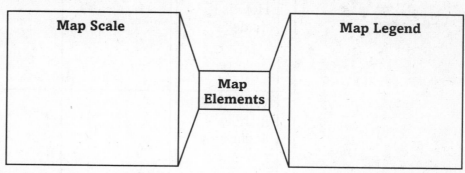

Map Scale

Map Elements

Map Legend

Geologic Maps

I found this information on page _____ .

Summarize *what* geologic maps *are and how they are used.*

_____
_____
_____
_____
_____

CONNECT IT If you were going to map your classroom, which map scale would be better: 1 cm:1 m or 1 cm: 10 m? Explain your reasoning.

_____
_____

Tie It Together

Model

Create a two-dimension physical map of your state in the space provided below. Include the major landforms found in your state. Use symbols to indicate these landforms on the map. Be sure to explain the symbols you use in a map legend. Your map should be proportional to the actual size of your state. Include a map scale to help others determine distances.

Views of Earth Chapter Wrap-Up

Now that you have read the chapter, think about what you have learned and complete the table below. Compare your previous answers with these.

1. Write an **A** if you agree with the statement.
2. Write a **D** if you disagree with the statement.

Views of Earth	After You Read
• All mountains form in the same way.	
• Lines of longitude run parallel to the equator.	
• All maps of Earth distort the shapes and sizes of landmasses.	

Review

Use this checklist to help you study.

☐ Review the information you included in your Foldable.

☐ Study your *Science Notebook* on this chapter.

☐ Study the definitions of vocabulary words.

☐ Review daily homework assignments.

☐ Re-read the chapter and review the charts, graphs, and illustrations.

☐ Review the Self Check at the end of each section.

☐ Look over the Chapter Review at the end of the chapter.

SUMMARIZE IT
Identify three important ideas in this chapter.

_____

_____

_____

_____

Weathering and Soil

Before You Read

Before you read the chapter, respond to these statements.

   1. Write an **A** if you agree with the statement.

   2. Write a **D** if you disagree with the statement.

Before You Read	Weathering and Soil
	• Plants can break apart rock.
	• Climate affects the rate at which soil forms.
	• Soil on steep slopes tends to be thicker than soil at the bottom of a slope.
	• Humans sometimes cause erosion to occur faster than new soil can form.

FOLDABLES™
Study Organizer

Construct the Foldable as directed at the beginning of this chapter.

Science Journal

A tor is a pile of boulders left on land after the surrounding, weakened rock is worn away. Write a poem about a tor. Use words in your poem that rhyme with the word tor.

_____

_____

_____

_____

_____

_____

Weathering and Soil
Section 1 Weathering

Scan *the headings of Section 1 to determine two main types of weathering that will be discussed.*

1. _____

2. _____

Review Vocabulary

Define surface area, *and use it in a scientific sentence.*

surface area

_____

_____

_____

_____

New Vocabulary

Read the definitions below. Write the key term on the blank in the left column.

_____ surface processes that break rock into smaller and smaller pieces

_____ physical processes that break rock apart without changing its chemical makeup

_____ mechanical weathering process that occurs when water freezes in the cracks in rock and expands

_____ process in which chemical reactions dissolve the minerals in rock or change them into different minerals

_____ chemical weathering process that occurs as minerals are exposed to air and water

_____ the long-term pattern of weather that occurs in a particular area

Academic Vocabulary

Use a dictionary to define the term process *as a noun.*

process

_____

_____

Name _____ **Date** _____

Section 1 Weathering (continued)

◁ Main Idea ▷

Weathering and Its Effects

I found this information on page _____.

Mechanical Weathering

I found this information on page _____.

◁ Details ▷

Sequence *the sediment grain types in order of size.*

Coarsest ⟶ Finest

[ ] ⟶ [ ] ⟶ [ ]

Organize *information by completing the outline below as you read.*

Mechanical Weathering

  I. Plants and Animals

    A. _____

    _____

    B. _____

    _____

  II. Ice Wedging

    A. _____

    B. _____

    _____

    C. _____

    _____

  III. Surface Area

    A. _____

    _____

    B. _____

    _____

    C. _____

    _____

Section 1 Weathering (continued)

Main Idea | Details

Chemical Weathering

I found this information on page _____ .

Sequence *steps to explain how carbon dioxide causes* chemical weathering.

Chemical Weathering by Carbonic Acid	
1.	
2.	
3.	
4.	

Effects of Climate

I found this information on page _____ .

Synthesize *the effects of climate and rock type on the rate of weathering in the table below.*

Factors that Affect the Rate of Weathering	
Factor	Effects
climate	Chemical weathering Mechanical weathering
rock type	

Analyze *how oxygen can cause chemical weathering. Discuss where you have seen* oxidation *around your home.*

_____

_____

_____

_____

_____

_____

Weathering and Soil
Section 2 The Nature of Soil

Predict *two things that might be discussed in this section on the basis of its title.*

1. _____

2. _____

Review Vocabulary **Define** *the term* profile.

profile _____

New Vocabulary *Use your book or a dictionary to define the following terms.*

soil _____
_____

humus _____
_____

horizon _____
_____

soil profile _____
_____

litter _____
_____

leaching _____
_____

Academic Vocabulary *Use a dictionary to define* indicate.

indicate _____

Section 2 The Nature of Soil (continued)

Main Idea

Formation of Soil

I found this information on page _____ .

Details

Complete *the graphic organizer to show the five factors that affect soil* formation.

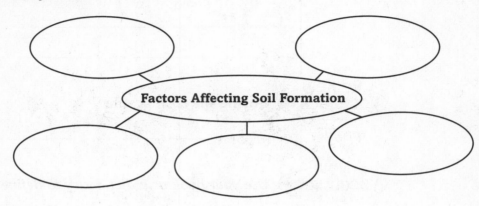

Composition of Soil

I found this information on page _____ .

Identify *the five components of soil, and create a symbol to represent each.*

Component of Soil					
My Soil Symbol					

I found this information on page _____ .

Compare and contrast *dry soil and moist soil. Create sketches in the top row, and write descriptions in the bottom row.*

Dry Soil	Moist Soil

Section 2 The Nature of Soil (continued)

Main Idea	Details
Soil Profile	**Model** *a soil profile by drawing and labeling it below.*

I found this information on page _____.

I found this information on page _____.

Organize *information about soil structure in the concept map.*

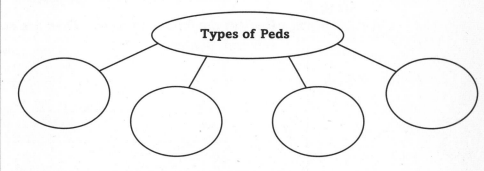

Soil Types

I found this information on page _____.

Summarize *information about how soil varies in different regions.*

Region	Soil
desert	
prairie	
temperate forest	

CONNECT IT Analyze relationships between organisms and soil. Describe how organisms use soil and how organisms affect soil.

_____

_____

_____

Weathering and Soil
Section 3 Soil Erosion

Skim *the headings and the boldfaced terms in Section 3. Identify three facts about soil erosion and ways to reduce its occurrence.*

1. _____

2. _____

3. _____

Review Vocabulary *Use* erosion *in a scientific sentence.*

erosion _____

New Vocabulary **Define** *the following terms. Then use each term in an original scientific sentence.*

no-till farming _____

_____

_____

_____

contour farming _____

_____

_____

_____

terracing _____

_____

_____

Academic Vocabulary *Define the term* compensate *as it refers to soil.*

compensate _____

Name _____ **Date** _____

Section 3 Soil Erosion (continued)

Main Idea	**Details**

Soil—An Important Resource

I found this information on page _____.

Evaluate *why* soil erosion *is a serious problem for agriculture.*

_____

_____

_____

_____

Causes and Effects of Soil Erosion

I found this information on page _____.

Organize *information on the causes and effects of soil erosion by completing the diagram below.*

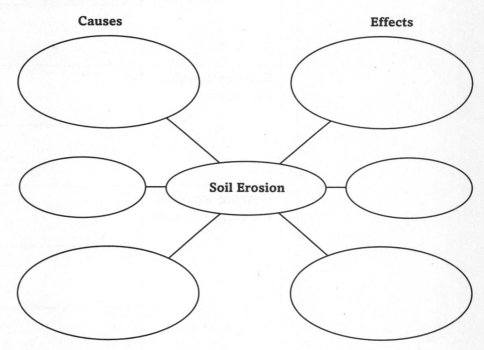

Causes   Effects

Soil Erosion

I found this information on page _____.

Identify *the causes and effects of excess sediment.*

Excess sediment

is caused by →

can affect →

Section 3 Soil Erosion (continued)

Main Idea

Preventing Soil Erosion

I found this information on page _____.

Details

Summarize *methods of preventing soil erosion.*

Preventing Soil Erosion	
Strategy	Methods
Manage crops	1.
	2.
	3.
Reduce erosion on slopes	1.
	2.
Reduce erosion on exposed soil	1.
	2.
	3.

CONNECT IT

Identify ways to prevent erosion that are probably used in your community and explain why they are used.

_____

_____

_____

_____

Tie It Together

Model

Recall evidence of erosion that you have seen in your community. Then create a model to demonstrate how the erosion probably occurred. You may make a working three-dimensional model that you can demonstrate for the class. You may represent your model with a labeled drawing. Describe how the model can be changed to prevent erosion.

Weathering and Soil Chapter Wrap-Up

Now that you have read the chapter, think about what you have learned and complete the table below. Compare your previous answers with these.

1. Write an **A** if you agree with the statement.
2. Write a **D** if you disagree with the statement.

Weathering and Soil	After You Read
• Plants can break apart rock.	
• Climate affects the rate at which soil forms.	
• Soil on steep slopes usually is thicker than soil at the bottom of a slope.	
• Humans sometimes cause erosion to occur faster than new soil can form.	

Review

Use this checklist to help you study.

- ☐ Review the information you included in your Foldable.
- ☐ Study your *Science Notebook* on this chapter.
- ☐ Study the definitions of vocabulary words.
- ☐ Review daily homework assignments.
- ☐ Re-read the chapter and review the charts, graphs, and illustrations.
- ☐ Review the Self Check at the end of each section.
- ☐ Look over the Chapter Review at the end of the chapter.

SUMMARIZE IT
After reading this chapter, identify three things that you have learned about weathering and soil.

_____

_____

_____

_____

Erosional Forces

Preview

Before you read the chapter, respond to these statements.

1. Write an **A** if you agree with the statement.
2. Write a **D** if you disagree with the statement.

Before You Read	Erosional Forces
	• Glaciers can erode rocks and soil.
	• Human activity can increase erosion.
	• Steep slopes can be unsafe for structures such as houses.
	• Planting vegetation can increase erosion.

 *Construct the Foldable as directed at the beginning of this chapter.*

Science Journal

Name three major landforms around the world. Hypothesize what erosional forces helped shape them. Use sketches to help you think about the processes.

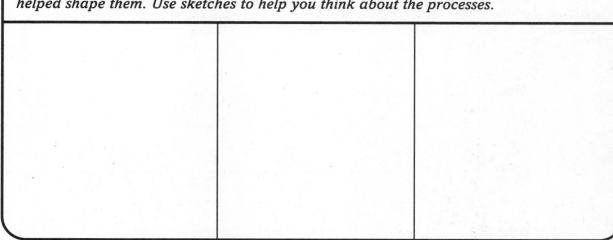

Erosional Forces
Section 1 Erosion by Gravity

Predict *what you will learn about* erosion *after looking at each illustration in Section 1 of your book.*

_____

_____

Review Vocabulary

Write a sentence using the word sediment *to show its scientific meaning.*

sediment

_____

_____

New Vocabulary

Define *the following key terms by using your book or a dictionary.*

erosion _____

_____

deposition _____

_____

mass movement _____

_____

slump _____

_____

creep _____

_____

Academic Vocabulary

Use a dictionary to define the word structure.

structure _____

_____

Name _____ Date _____

Section 1 Erosion by Gravity (continued)

Main Idea	**Details**
Erosion and Deposition	**Identify** *four major agents of* erosion.
I found this information on page _____.	1. _____
	2. _____
	3. _____
	4. _____
	Summarize *how energy affects the ability of agents of erosion to carry and drop sediment. Then describe how this occurs with water.*
	_____
	_____
	_____
	Water: _____
	_____
	_____
Mass Movement	**Compare and contrast** *characteristics of* mass movements *by completing the following chart.*
I found this information on page _____.	

Mass Movements	
Types	**Description**
Slump	
	A mixture of sediment and water flows down a slope.
Rock slide	
Creep	
	Blocks of rock break loose and tumble through the air.

Section 1 Erosion by Gravity (continued)

Main Idea	Details
I found this information on page _____.	**Model** *what a slope would look like before and after a mudflow.*

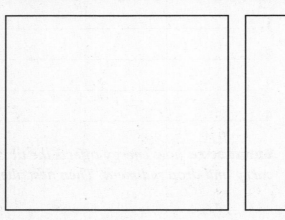

Before   After

Consequences of Erosion

I found this information on page _____.

Analyze *ways to reduce erosion on steep slopes. Complete the graphic organizer below.*

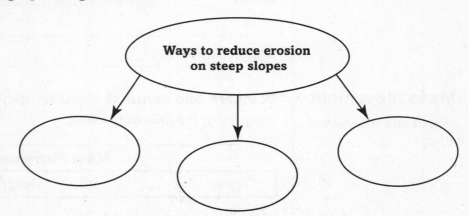

COMPARE IT Model a way to build a house on a hillside. Draw the house and show methods to protect the house from erosion caused by gravity.

Erosional Forces
Section 2 Glaciers

Scan *the illustration headings in Section 2. Write three true statements about glaciers on the lines below.*

_____

_____

_____

_____

Review Vocabulary

Define plasticlike *using your book.*

plasticlike

_____

_____

New Vocabulary

Write a scientific sentence for each vocabulary word.

glacier

_____

_____

plucking

_____

_____

till

_____

_____

moraine

_____

_____

outwash

_____

_____

Academic Vocabulary

Define accumulate *by using a dictionary.*

accumulate

_____

Section 2 **Glaciers** (continued)

Main Idea — Details

How Glaciers Form and Move

I found this information on page _____.

Sequence *the steps of* glacier *formation and movement. The first step has been completed for you.*

1. When snow doesn't melt, it piles up.

2. _____

_____

3. _____

4. _____

Ice Eroding Rock

I found this information on page _____.

Contrast *two ways that glaciers erode rock.*

Plucking	Scouring

Ice Depositing Sediment

I found this information on page _____.

Summarize *the types of glacier deposits in the chart below.*

Mass Movements			
Type	Consists of	Deposited by	Example of landform that is left behind
Till			
Outwash			

Section 2 Glaciers (continued)

Main Idea	Details

Continental Glaciers

I found this information on page _____.

Identify *key facts about* continental glaciers. *Complete the concept map below.*

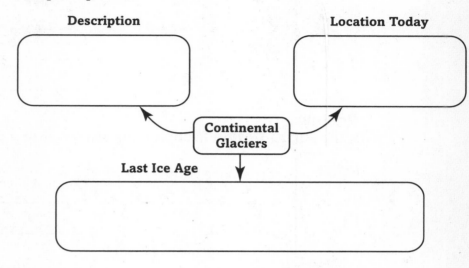

Valley Glaciers

I found this information on page _____.

Create *a labeled diagram of a mountain that has been eroded by* valley glaciers.

SYNTHESIZE IT Outside of a town in the Midwest is a long, winding ridge made of sand and gravel. Hypothesize how this landform may have formed.

_____

_____

_____

Erosional Forces
Section 3 Wind

Skim *the headings in Section 3. Write three questions that occur to you.*

1. _____

2. _____

3. _____

Review Vocabulary

Define friction *using your book or a dictionary.*

friction

_____

_____

_____

New Vocabulary

Read each definition. Write the correct vocabulary word to match on the blank in the left column.

_____ when windblown sediment strikes rock, the surface of the rock gets scraped and worn away

_____ wind-blown deposits of fine-grained sediments are called

_____ a mound of sand drifted by the wind.

_____ wind removes small particles such as silt and sand and leaves behind heavier, coarser material.

Academic Vocabulary

Write a sentence that shows the meaning of the word eventual.

eventual

_____

_____

Name _____ **Date** _____

Section 3 Wind (continued)

Main Idea   **Details**

Wind Erosion

I found this information on page _____.

Contrast *two ways wind differs from other agents of erosion.*

1. _____

_____

2. _____

_____

Sequence deflation *and* abrasion *in the flowchart. Make a sketch for the process that occurs in each box.*

Deflation	Abrasion
Drawing	Drawing
Description	Description

I found this information on page _____.

Contrast *sandstorms and dust storms in the chart.*

	Sandstorms	Dust Storms
What particles are carried by the storm?		
What happens?		

Section 3 Wind (continued)

Main Idea / Details

Reducing Wind Erosion

I found this information on page _____.

Summarize *how plants help conserve soil. Make a sketch to show each effect in the boxes at right.*

1. Windbreaks: _____

_____

_____

_____

_____

2. Roots: _____

_____

_____

_____

_____

Deposition by Wind

I found this information on page _____.

Complete *the statements about* loess *and sand* dunes.

Loess forms when wind blows across _____. When

the sediment is dropped, it forms _____

deposits. Loess deposits often become _____ soils. Sand dunes

often form in _____. After the dunes form, they move in the

direction that the _____ blows. Sand blows up the _____

side of the dune. It then falls down the _____ side of the dune.

This process causes the _____ to move slowly across the desert.

SYNTHESIZE IT

During the 1930s, wind eroded soil from much of the south-central United States (the Dust Bowl). Infer what farming practices might have contributed to the Dust Bowl. Summarize how farmers could have protected their farms.

_____

_____

_____

Tie It Together

Plan Articles

Imagine that you are a reporter for a newspaper. The town where you live is located near a moraine and along the shore of a large lake. Plan a series of two articles that will explain

    i. how erosion and deposition shaped the town's land

    ii. what dangers the town may face from erosion in the future.

Article 1

Topic: Erosion and deposition and the town's history

Headline: _____

Key Points for Article:

_____

_____

_____

_____

_____

_____

_____

Article 2

Topic: Mass wasting

Headline: _____

Key Points for Article:

_____

_____

_____

_____

_____

_____

Erosional Forces Chapter Wrap-Up

Now that you have read the chapter, think about what you have learned and complete the table below. Compare your previous answers with these.

1. Write an **A** if you agree with the statement.
2. Write a **D** if you disagree with the statement.

Erosional Forces	After You Read
• Glaciers can erode rocks and soil.	
• Human activity can increase erosion.	
• Steep slopes can be unsafe for structures such as houses.	
• Planting vegetation can increase erosion.	

Review

Use this checklist to help you study.

- ☐ Review the information you included in your Foldable.
- ☐ Study your *Science Notebook* on this chapter.
- ☐ Study the definitions of vocabulary words.
- ☐ Review daily homework assignments.
- ☐ Re-read the chapter and review the charts, graphs, and illustrations.
- ☐ Review the Self Check at the end of each section.
- ☐ Look over the Chapter Review at the end of the chapter.

SUMMARIZE IT After reading this chapter, identify three things that you have learned about erosional forces.

_____

_____

_____

_____

Name _____ Date _____

Water Erosion and Deposition

Before You Read

Before you read the chapter, respond to these statements.

1. Write an **A** if you agree with the statement.
2. Write a **D** if you disagree with the statement.

Before You Read	Water Erosion and Deposition
	• The presence of plants can affect how much water runs off the land.
	• When a river forms, its course never changes.
	• Water that soaks into the ground becomes part of a system, just as water above ground does.
	• Beaches are always made of pieces of rock.

 *Construct the Foldable as directed at the beginning of this chapter.*

Science Journal

Hoodoos are narrow towers of rock. What processes might have formed hoodoos? What will happen if this process continues?

_____

_____

_____

_____

_____

_____

_____

Water Erosion and Deposition
Section 1 Surface Water

Skim *Section 1 of your book and read the headings. Write three questions that come to mind. Try to answer your questions as you read.*

1. _____

2. _____

3. _____

Review Vocabulary

Define erosion.

erosion

_____

_____

_____

New Vocabulary

Write a paragraph that uses each vocabulary term in a way that shows its scientific meaning.

runoff

drainage basin

meander

_____

_____

_____

_____

_____

_____

_____

Academic Vocabulary

Use your book or a dictionary to define likewise.

likewise

_____

Section 1 Surface Water (continued)

<Main Idea>   <Details>

Runoff

I found this information on page _____ .

Distinguish *four factors that determine how much* runoff *occurs after rain falls.*

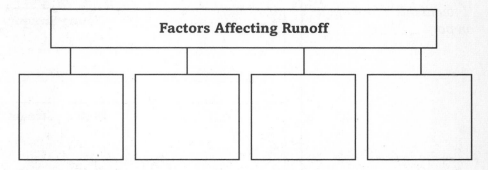

Water Erosion

I found this information on page _____ .

Summarize *the causes and effects of four types of surface water erosion in the chart below.*

Type	Causes	Effects
Rill		
Gully		
Sheet		
Stream		

River System Development

I found this information on page _____ .

Scan *the map of* drainage basins *in the United States in your text. Identify three major drainage basins.*

1. _____

2. _____

3. _____

Section 1 Surface Water (continued)

⟨ Main Idea ⟩   ⟨ Details ⟩

Stages of Stream Development

I found this information on page _____.

Sequence *the stages of stream development. Complete the flow chart to identify the key features of each stage.*

Young Streams

↓

Mature Streams

↓

Old Streams

Too Much Water

I found this information on page _____.

Contrast *the roles and locations of* dams *and* levees.

_____

_____

_____

Deposition by Surface Water

I found this information on page _____.

Summarize *how rivers deposit sediments. Describe how* deltas *and* alluvial fans *form.*

As water slows, it _____.

These deposits form a delta when _____

_____. They form an alluvial fan when _____

_____.

SYNTHESIZE IT   A broad, flat river flows slowly along its bed while a young, swift stream rushes past. Explain which one would probably deposit more sediment.

_____

_____

Water Erosion and Deposition

Water Erosion and Deposition
Section 2 Groundwater

Scan the headings in Section 2. Then predict three topics that will be covered in this section.

1. _____

2. _____

3. _____

Review Vocabulary **Define** pore.

pore
_____

_____

New Vocabulary *Use your book to define the following terms.*

permeable
_____

_____

aquifer
_____

_____

water table
_____

_____

geyser
_____

_____

Academic Vocabulary *Use your book or a dictionary to define* underlie.

underlie
_____

Section 2 Groundwater (continued)

⟨ **Main Idea** ⟩   _____⟨ **Details** ⟩_____

Groundwater Systems

I found this information on page _____ .

I found this information on page _____ .

Summarize *how* groundwater *collects. Complete the graphic organizer.*

Soil is made of fragments of rocks and minerals with spaces between them.	→	

Create *a drawing that shows how groundwater flows. Label the impermeable layer, permeable layer, water table, and zone of saturation. Use arrows to show how the groundwater flows.*

Water Table

I found this information on page _____ .

Organize *information about* wells *and* springs. *Complete the chart.*

Water Source	Important Features
Regular well	
Artesian well	
Spring	

Name _____ **Date** _____

Section 2 Groundwater (continued)

⟨ **Main Idea** ⟩	⟨ **Details** ⟩

Water Table

I found this information on page _____.

Sequence *the events that cause a* geyser *to erupt. Complete the flow chart.*

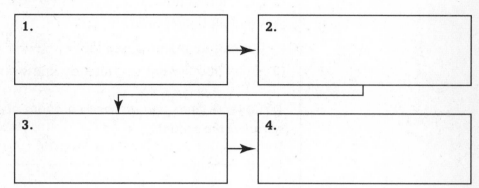

The Work of Groundwater

I found this information on page _____.

Complete *the concept map to identify ways that groundwater shapes land.*

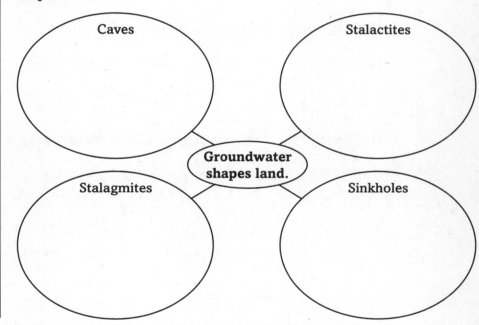

CONNECT IT Aquifers are important natural resources. Due to human activity, the levels of some aquifers have dropped over time. What problems can this cause for humans?

_____

_____

_____

Water Erosion and Deposition
Section 3 Ocean Shoreline

Scan *Section 3 of your text using the checklist below.*

☐ Read all section titles.

☐ Read all bold words.

☐ Look at all pictures and labels.

☐ Think about what you already know about waves and shorelines.

Write three facts you discovered about ocean shorelines as you scanned the section.

1. _____

2. _____

3. _____

 **Define** spring tide.

spring tide _____

_____

 *Use your book to define the following terms.*

longshore current _____

_____

beach _____

_____

 *Use your book or a dictionary to find the meaning of* transport *as a verb. Then write a sentence using the term.*

transport _____

_____

Section 3 Ocean Shoreline (continued)

Main Idea

Details

The Shore

I found this information on page _____.

Complete *the graphic organizer below to identify how* shoreline erosion *occurs.*

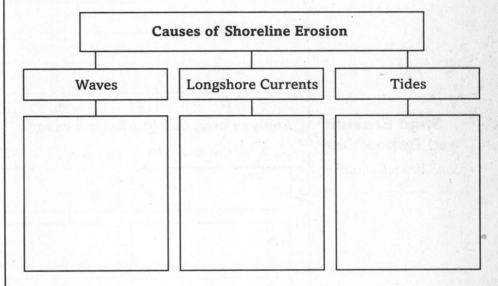

Rocky Shorelines

I found this information on page _____.

Sequence *three steps in the erosion process of a rocky shoreline. Create a sketch to help you remember each step.*

1.	
2.	
3.	

Section 3 Ocean Shoreline (continued)

Main Idea   **Details**

Sandy Beaches

I found this information on page _____.

Summarize *how* beach sand *forms*.

_____
_____
_____
_____

Sand Erosion and Deposition

I found this information on page _____.

Analyze *ways that beaches can change.*

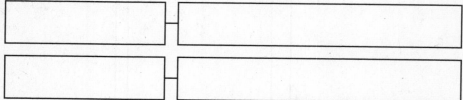

Cause   Effect

Analyze *how* barrier islands *form and change. Complete the outline.*

   I. How barrier islands form

   A. _____

   B. _____

   II. How barrier islands change

   A. _____

   B. _____

SYNTHESIZE IT Which shoreline feature would you expect to last longest: a rocky shoreline, a sandy beach, or a barrier island? Which would you expect to last the shortest time? Explain your response.

_____
_____
_____

Tie It Together

Test Soil Permeability

In a small group, collect several different types of soil or rock, such as gravel, sand, and clay. Test the permeability of each sample by following the process below.

1. Cut the top from a plastic 2-liter bottle. Be sure to follow safety procedures when cutting.

2. Place about 10 cm of the material to be tested in the bottom part of the bottle.

3. Pour 100 ml of water into the bottle. Use a stopwatch to determine how long it takes the water to soak into the material. Observe the substance carefully until there is no water collected on the surface of the soil or gravel.

4. Record your results in the table below.

5. Remove the material from the bottle, and rinse and dry the bottle thoroughly. Then repeat steps 1–4 with the other materials you chose.

Material	Time

Given your results, which material would you use in the yard of a house built on a low area? Explain your response.

_____

_____

_____

_____

_____

Water Erosion and Deposition
Chapter Wrap-Up

Now that you have read the chapter, think about what you have learned and complete the table below. Compare your previous answers with these.

1. Write an **A** if you agree with the statement.
2. Write a **D** if you disagree with the statement.

Water Erosion and Deposition	After You Read
• The presence of plants can affect how much water runs off the land.	
• When a river forms, its course never changes.	
• Water that soaks into the ground becomes part of a system, just as water above ground does.	
• Beaches are always made of pieces of rock.	

Review

Use this checklist to help you study.

☐ Review the information you included in your Foldable.

☐ Study your *Science Notebook* on this chapter.

☐ Study the definitions of vocabulary words.

☐ Review daily homework assignments.

☐ Re-read the chapter and review the charts, graphs, and illustrations.

☐ Review the Self Check at the end of each section.

☐ Look over the Chapter Review at the end of the chapter.

SUMMARIZE IT
After reading this chapter, identify three things that you have learned about erosion and deposition by water.

_____

_____

_____

Name _____ **Date** _____

Plate Tectonics

Before You Read

Before you read the chapter, respond to these statements.

1. Write an **A** if you agree with the statement.
2. Write a **D** if you disagree with the statement.

Before You Read	Plate Tectonics
	• Fossil evidence provides support for the idea that continents have moved over time.
	• New seafloor is continuously forming while old seafloor is being destroyed.
	• Earth's crust is broken into sections called plates.
	• Rock flows deep inside Earth.

Construct the Foldable as directed at the beginning of this chapter.

Science Journal

Pretend you're a journalist with an audience that assumes the continents have never moved. Write about the kinds of evidence you'll need to convince people otherwise.

_____

_____

_____

_____

_____

_____

_____

Plate Tectonics
Section 1 Continental Drift

Skim *through Section 1 of your book. Write three questions that come to mind from reading the headings and examining the illustrations.*

1. _____

_____

2. _____

_____

3. _____

_____

Define continent *to show its scientific meaning.*

continent _____

_____

Use your book to define the following terms. Then write an original sentence using each term.

continental drift _____

_____

_____

_____

Pangaea _____

_____

_____

Use a dictionary to define controversy.

controversy _____

_____

Section 1 Continental Drift (continued)

Main Idea | ## Details

Evidence for Continental Drift

I found this information on page _____.

Summarize Alfred Wegener's hypothesis *about Earth's continents.*

_____
_____
_____
_____
_____

I found this information on page _____.

Create *a graphic organizer to identify the three types of clues that are evidence for* continental drift.

I found this information on page _____.

Analyze *the clue in the left column below. Then describe how Alfred Wegener would have explained it in the right column.*

Clue	Wegener's Response
Fossils of Mesosaurus found in South America and Africa	
Fossil plant found in five continents, including Antarctica	
Fossils of warm weather plants found on Arctic island	
Glacial deposits found in Afric, India, and Australia	

Section 1 Continental Drift (continued)

Main Idea

I found this information on page _____.

Details

Model *what the continents may have looked like 250 million years ago.*

[ ]

How could continents drift?

I found this information on page _____.

Summarize *Wegener's explanations of how and why continental drift occurs.*

Wegener's explanation for continental drift

How: _____

_____

Why: _____

_____

EVALUATE IT

Do you think it was reasonable for scientists initially to reject the hypothesis of continental drift? Explain your response.

_____

_____

_____

_____

Plate Tectonics
Section 2 Seafloor Spreading

Predict *three things that might be discussed in Section 2 after reading its headings.*

1. _____

2. _____

3. _____

Review Vocabulary

Define seafloor. *Then use the word in a sentence.*

seafloor

_____

_____

_____

_____

New Vocabulary

Use your book to define seafloor spreading. *Then use the term in a sentence.*

seafloor spreading

_____

_____

_____

_____

Academic Vocabulary

Use a dictionary to define interval. *Then use the word in a sentence about magnetic clues to seafloor spreading.*

interval

_____

_____

_____

_____

Section 2 Seafloor Spreading (continued)

Main Idea

Details

Mapping the Ocean Floor

_I found this information on page _____._

Summarize *how sound waves are used to map the seafloor.*

_____

_____

_____

_____

_____

_I found this information on page _____._

Model *the process of* seafloor spreading *by drawing a cross section of a mid-ocean ridge and the magma below it. Use arrows to indicate the directions of motion.*

Sequence *steps describing seafloor spreading.*

Hot, less dense material below Earth's crust rises toward the surface at a mid-ocean ridge.

The less dense material flows _____ _____.

As the seafloor spreads apart, magma is _____ _____.

Section 2 Seafloor Spreading (continued)

⌐Main Idea⌐	⌐Details⌐

Evidence for Spreading

I found this information on page _____.

Label *the diagram below to identify evidence for seafloor spreading. Add arrows to show the direction of spreading, and indicate where older rock and newer rock occur.*

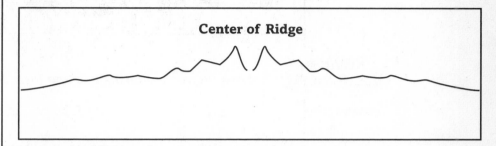

Center of Ridge

I found this information on page _____.

Model *the polarity of Earth's magnetic field today.*

• Draw a sphere to represent Earth.

• Label the north pole and south pole.

• Draw arrows indicating the direction in which magnetic lines of force enter and leave Earth.

Summarize *how reversals in the direction of Earth's magnetic field have provided evidence of seafloor spreading.*

At times, the _____ that pass

through Earth have _____. _____ of

Earth's magnetic field are recorded in _____ that forms

along _____. Scientists can detect

_____ that are _____ to mid-ocean

ridges. This occurs on _____.

Plate Tectonics
Section 3 Theory of Plate Tectonics

Scan *the headings and illustrations in Section 3. List four features caused by plate tectonics.*

1. _____   3. _____

2. _____   4. _____

Review Vocabulary

Define *the review terms to show their scientific meanings.*

converge _____

diverge _____

transform _____

New Vocabulary

Use your book to define the following terms.

plate _____

_____

plate tectonics _____

_____

lithosphere _____

_____

asthenosphere _____

_____

convection current _____

_____

Academic Vocabulary

Use a dictionary to define rigid.

rigid _____

_____

Copyright © Glencoe/McGraw-Hill, a division of The McGraw-Hill Companies, Inc.

Section 3 Theory of Plate Tectonics (continued)

Main Idea	Details

Plate Tectonics

I found this information on page _____.

Complete *the following outline on the theory of* plate tectonics.

I. A new theory

   A. In the 1960s, a new theory called _____ was developed.

   B. Earth's _____ and part of the _____

   are broken into sections called _____, that move slowly.

II. Details about the theory

   A. The layer of Earth that is broken into sections is called

   the _____.

   B. The _____ is the plasticlike layer below the

   _____.

   C. The rigid plates move over the _____.

Plate Boundaries

I found this information on page _____.

Compare and contrast *the different plate boundaries by defining them side by side. Draw the plates of the world. Identify plate motion by using arrows.*

Divergent	Convergent	Transform

Section 3 Theory of Plate Tectonics (continued)

Main Idea

Details

Causes of Plate Tectonics

I found this information on page _____.

Label *the convection currents depicted below with heating, rising, cooling, and sinking.*

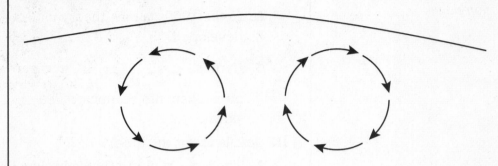

Features Caused by Plate Tectonics

I found this information on page _____.

Organize *information to describe features caused by plate tectonics. Fill in the chart below.*

Feature	Description
Rift valley	
Folded and faulted mountains	
Strike-slip faults	

Testing for Plate Tectonics

I found this information on page _____.

Summarize *how the Satellite Laser Ranging System measures plate movement.*

_____

_____

_____

_____

Name _____ Date _____

Tie It Together

Synthesize It

Your book has a picture showing how continents may have drifted. It shows their positions 250 million years ago, 125 million years ago, and at the present. Work with a partner to trace the paths that the continents have taken. Then extend their paths forward in time to project where they may be 125 million years from now. Draw a map in the space below, showing your prediction.

Plate Tectonics Chapter Wrap-Up

Now that you have read the chapter, think about what you have learned and complete the table below. Compare your previous answers with these.

    1. Write an **A** if you agree with the statement.

    2. Write a **D** if you disagree with the statement.

Plate Tectonics	After You Read
• Fossil evidence provides support for the idea that continents have moved over time.	
• New seafloor is continuously forming while old seafloor is being destroyed.	
• Earth's crust is broken into sections called plates.	
• Rock flows deep inside Earth.	

Review

Use this checklist to help you study.

☐ Review the information you included in your Foldable.

☐ Study your *Science Notebook* on this chapter.

☐ Study the definitions of vocabulary words.

☐ Review daily homework assignments.

☐ Re-read the chapter and review the charts, graphs, and illustrations.

☐ Review the Self Check at the end of each section.

☐ Look over the Chapter Review at the end of the chapter.

SUMMARIZE IT After reading this chapter, identify three things that you have learned about plate tectonics.

_____

_____

_____

_____

Earthquakes

Before You Read

Before you read the chapter, respond to these statements.

1. Write an **A** if you agree with the statement.
2. Write a **D** if you disagree with the statement.

Before You Read	Earthquakes
	• Earthquakes release energy.
	• The interior of Earth has several layers.
	• Earthquake waves travel through all parts of Earth at the same speed.
	• Thousands of earthquakes occur on Earth every day.

Construct the Foldable as directed at the beginning of this chapter.

Science Journal

Write three things that you would ask a scientist studying earthquakes.

_____

_____

_____

_____

_____

_____

Earthquakes
Section 1 Forces Inside Earth

Preview *the headings in Section 1. Write three topics that you predict will be covered in this section.*

1. _____

2. _____

3. _____

Define plate *to show its scientific meaning.*

plate

_____

_____

Write the correct vocabulary term next to each definition.

_____ surface along which rocks move when they break

_____ vibrations caused by the breaking of rock

_____ fault in which rock above the fault surface moves downward in relation to rock below the fault surface

_____ fault in which rock above the fault surface is forced up and over the rock below the fault surface

_____ fault in which rocks on either side of the fault are moving past each other without much upward or downward motion

Write an original sentence that uses the term stress *and shows its scientific meaning.*

stress

_____

_____

Name _____ **Date** _____

Section 1 **Forces Inside Earth** (continued)

Main Idea

Details

Earthquake Causes

I found this information on page _____ .

Define *the* elastic limit *of an object.*

_____

_____

_____

I found this information on page _____ .

Summarize *how motion along faults causes* earthquakes.

_____

_____

_____

_____

_____

_____

_____

_____

Types of Faults

I found this information on page _____ .

Distinguish *the three types of forces that act on rocks. Complete the graphic organizer.*

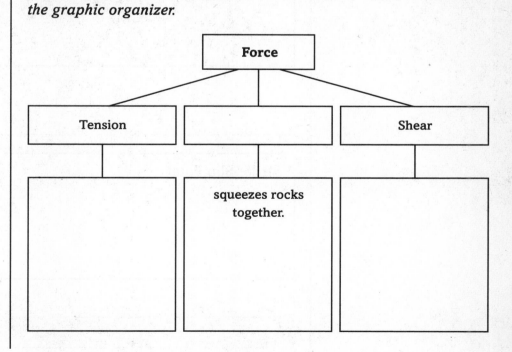

Force

Tension   squeezes rocks together.   Shear

Section 1 Forces Inside Earth (continued)

‹Main Idea› _____ **‹Details›** _____

I found this information on page _____.

Model *each type of fault.*

- Draw each type of fault.

- Include labeled arrows to show direction of motion.

- Draw and label another set of arrows to identify the type of force involved.

- Beneath each drawing, write a description of the fault.

Normal Fault

_____

Reverse Fault

_____

Strike-Slip Fault

_____

Earthquakes
Section 2 Features of Earthquakes

Read *the* What You'll Learn *statements. Rewrite each as a question. Then look for the answers as you read.*

1. _____

2. _____

3. _____

Review Vocabulary **Define** wave *to show its scientific meaning.*

wave

_____

_____

New Vocabulary *Write a paragraph about earthquakes, using the new vocabulary terms. Underline each vocabulary term as you use it.*

seismic wave _____

_____

focus _____

_____

primary wave _____

_____

secondary wave _____

_____

surface wave _____

_____

epicenter _____

_____

seismograph _____

Academic Vocabulary *Use a dictionary to define* exceed *to show its scientific meaning.*

exceed _____

_____

Name _____ Date _____

Section 2 Features of Earthquakes (continued)

Seismic Waves

I found this information on page _____.

Sequence *the process through which* seismic waves *form.*

1. Moving rocks get caught on each other at faults.

2. _____

3. _____

4. _____

I found this information on page _____.

Organize *information about the three types of seismic waves.*
Identify and explain how each wave moves.

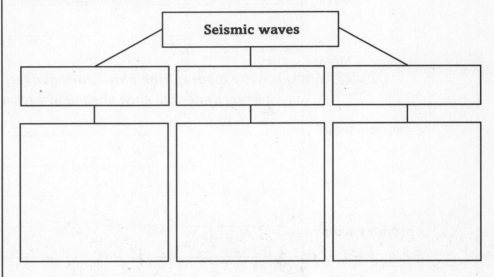

Summarize *which type of wave causes the most earthquake*
damage, and explain why.

Most earthquake damage is caused by _____ because

_____

_____ .

Locating an Epicenter

I found this information on page _____.

Analyze *the three types of seismic waves. Fill in the missing words.*

_____ are the fastest seismic waves, followed by

_____, which travel about _____ as fast.

_____ are the slowest seismic waves. If the epicenter

of an earthquake is far away, _____ arrive first.

Section 2 Features of Earthquakes (continued)

Main Idea	Details

I found this information on page _____.

Analyze *how* seismograms *are used to locate an earthquake's* epicenter.

_____

_____

_____

_____

_____

Basic Structure of Earth

I found this information on page _____.

Model *the structure of Earth. Draw and label the five layers.*

Analyze *how scientists use seismic waves to determine Earth's structure.*

_____

_____

_____

SYNTHESIZE IT

A scientist finds that primary waves from an earthquake arrived at a seismograph, but secondary waves did not. What can the scientist conclude about the path the waves took?

_____

Earthquakes
Section 3 People and Earthquakes

Skim *Section 3 of your book. Write down three questions that come to mind from reading the headings and examining the pictures and illustrations.*

1. _____

   _____

2. _____

   _____

3. _____

   _____

Review Vocabulary

Define crest *to show its scientific meaning in relation to waves.*

crest _____

_____

New Vocabulary

Use your book to define each vocabulary term.

magnitude _____

_____

liquefaction _____

_____

tsunami _____

_____

Academic Vocabulary

Use a dictionary to define detect *to show its scientific meaning.*

detect _____

_____

Section 3 People and Earthquakes (continued)

Main Idea	Details

Earthquake Activity

I found this information on page _____ .

Summarize *information about how earthquakes affect humans by listing one positive and one negative effect.*

Positive: _____

_____

Negative: _____

_____

I found this information on page _____ .

Distinguish *how the* Richter scale *represents the energy released by an earthquake and the height of the lines on a seismogram.*

For every increase of 1.0 on the Richter scale

the height of a line on a seismogram is	
	32 times greater

I found this information on page _____ .

Evaluate *how different magnitude earthquakes affect humans and cause damage.*

Richter scale magnitude	1.5	4.0	8.5
Felt by humans?			
Causes damage?			

I found this information on page _____ .

Distinguish *the four factors that can affect how much damage an earthquake causes.*

1. _____

2. _____

3. _____

4. _____

Name _____ Date _____

Main Idea

Details

I found this information on page _____.

Define *the* Mercalli scale *by identifying what it describes.*

The Mercalli scale describes _____

_____

Analyze *how* liquefaction *occurs and how it damages buildings.*

_____

_____

_____

I found this information on page _____.

Sequence *the events that result in a* tsunami.

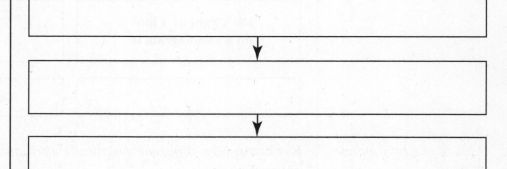

Earthquake Safety

I found this information on page _____.

Analyze *earthquake safety. List three ways to make a home more earthquake-safe.*

1. _____

2. _____

3. _____

CONNECT IT Look at the map in your book showing the risk of damaging earthquakes. What is the risk in your area? Draw a conclusion about the places where the risk is highest.

_____

_____

Tie It Together

Modeling

Construct a model of a building that is designed to resist earthquake damage. Present your model to the class, and explain how it protects against earthquake damage. Plan your model in the space below.

_____

_____

_____

_____

_____

_____

_____

_____

_____

_____

_____

_____

_____

_____

_____

_____

_____

_____

Earthquakes Chapter Wrap-Up

Now that you have read the chapter, think about what you have learned and complete the table below. Compare your previous answers with these.

1. Write an **A** if you agree with the statement.
2. Write a **D** if you disagree with the statement.

Earthquakes	After You Read
• Earthquakes release energy.	
• The interior of Earth has several layers.	
• Earthquake waves travel through all parts of Earth at the same speed.	
• Thousands of earthquakes occur on Earth every day.	

Review

Use this checklist to help you study.

☐ Review the information you included in your Foldable.

☐ Study your *Science Notebook* on this chapter.

☐ Study the definitions of vocabulary words.

☐ Review daily homework assignments.

☐ Re-read the chapter and review the charts, graphs, and illustrations.

☐ Review the Self Check at the end of each section.

☐ Look over the Chapter Review at the end of the chapter.

SUMMARIZE IT

After reading this chapter, identify three things that you have learned about earthquakes.

_____

_____

_____

_____

Volcanoes

Before You Read

Before you read the chapter, respond to these statements.

　1. Write an **A** if you agree with the statement.

　2. Write a **D** if you disagree with the statement.

Before You Read	Volcanoes
	• One volcano in Hawaii has been erupting for hundreds of years.
	• Lava is called magma when it reaches Earth's surface.
	• All volcanoes have the same type of eruptions.
	• Volcanic activity can form underground rock features.

 *Construct the Foldable as directed at the beginning of this chapter.*

Science Journal

Do all volcanoes begin with violent, explosive eruptions? Write about your current beliefs, then do some research and write about your discoveries.

_____

_____

_____

_____

_____

_____

_____

Volcanoes

Section 1 Volcanoes and Earth's Moving Plates

Predict three topics that might be discussed in Section 1 as you scan the headings and look at the pictures.

1. _____

2. _____

3. _____

Review Vocabulary **Define** lava.

lava
_____
_____

New Vocabulary *Use your book to define each vocabulary term.*

volcano
_____
_____

vent
_____
_____

crater
_____
_____

hot spot
_____
_____

Academic Vocabulary *Use a dictionary to define* **area** *as it is used in geography.*

area
_____
_____

Section 1 Volcanoes and Earth's Moving Plates (continued)

Main Idea	Details

What are volcanoes?

I found this information on page _____.

Identify *two places on Earth that have* active volcanoes.

1. _____

2. _____

Effects of Eruptions

I found this information on page _____.

Summarize *the effects of* volcanic eruptions *on people.*

Product of Eruption	Effect on People
Lava	
Ash	
Pyroclastic flow	
Sulfurous gas	

How do volcanoes form?

I found this information on page _____.

Sequence *the events that occur as a volcano forms.*

↓

↓

↓

Section 1 Volcanoes and Earth's Moving Plates (continued)

Main Idea

Details

Where do volcanoes occur?

I found this information on page _____.

Identify *the three places at which volcanoes often form.*

1. _____

2. _____

3. _____

I found this information on page _____.

Compare and contrast *how volcanoes form at* divergent *and* convergent *plate boundaries.*

At Divergent Boundary	At Convergent Boundary

I found this information on page _____.

Sequence *the events that caused the Hawaiian Islands to form.*

An area between Earth's core and mantle was unusually hot.	→	

↓

	→	

CONNECT IT

Look at the map of volcanoes and plate boundaries in your book. Describe where most volcanoes occur.

_____

_____

Volcanoes
Section 2 Types of Volcanoes

Skim *Section 2 of your book. Write three questions that come to mind as you read the headings and examine the illustrations. Look for the answers as you read.*

1. _____

2. _____

3. _____

Review Vocabulary **Define** magma.

magma | _____

_____

New Vocabulary *Use your book to define each vocabulary term.*

shield volcano | _____

_____

tephra | _____

_____

cinder cone volcano | _____

_____

composite volcano | _____

_____

Academic Vocabulary *Use a dictionary to define* release *as a verb.*

release | _____

_____

Section 2 Types of Volcanoes (continued)

Main Idea

Details

What controls eruptions?

I found this information on page _____.

Identify *the effects of trapped gases on volcanic eruptions.*

Cause		Effect on Eruption
Gases escape easily from magma.	→	
Gases build up to high pressures in magma.	→	

Composition of Magma

I found this information on page _____.

Contrast pahoehoe *lava and* aa *lava.*

Pahoehoe lava _____

_____

Aa lava _____

_____

Compare and contrast *the three major types of magma. Identify the characteristics of each type and the type of volcanic eruption to which each leads.*

	Basaltic	Granitic	Andesitic
Silica content			
Where it is found			
Type of eruption			

Section 2 Types of Volcanoes (continued)

Main Idea

Forms of Volcanoes

I found this information on page _____.

Details

Organize *information about the three types of volcanoes. Complete the graphic organizer.*

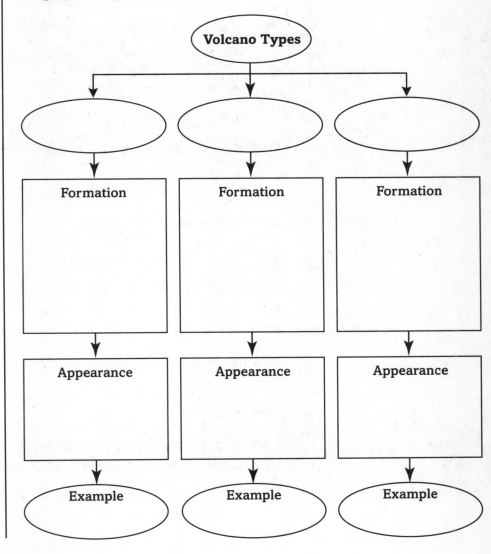

Volcano Types

Formation

Formation

Formation

Appearance

Appearance

Appearance

Example

Example

Example

SUMMARIZE IT

Describe two factors that control whether an eruption will be quiet or explosive.

_____

_____

_____

_____

Volcanoes
Section 3 Igneous Rock Features

Scan *the section headings, boldfaced words, and illustrations. Write three facts that you discovered about rock features.*

1. _____

   _____

2. _____

   _____

3. _____

   _____

Review Vocabulary **Define** intrude *and* extrude.

intrude _____

extrude _____

New Vocabulary *Write the vocabulary term that matches each definition.*

_____ one of the largest intrusive igneous rock bodies

_____ magma that is forced into a crack that cuts across rock layers and hardens

_____ igneous rock feature formed when magma is squeezed into a horizontal crack between layers of rock and then hardens underground

_____ solid igneous core left behind when a volcano erodes

_____ depression left when the top of a volcano collapses

Academic Vocabulary *Use a dictionary to define* collapse.

collapse _____

_____

Section 3 Igneous Rock Features (continued)

Main Idea

Intrusive Features

I found this information on page _____.

I found this information on page _____.

Details

Define intrusive rock *features. Then identify the four most common types of intrusive features.*

Intrusive rock features are _____

_____

_____ .

Compare and contrast batholiths, dikes, *and* sills *by completing the chart below.*

Feature	Origin, Size, and Shape
Batholiths	
Dikes	
Sills	

Section 3 Igneous Rock Features (continued)

Main Idea

Other Features

I found this information on page _____.

I found this information on page _____.

Details

Sequence *events to explain how a* volcanic neck *forms.*

1. _____

2. _____

3. _____

4. _____

Model *the stages of caldera formation by drawing three pictures.*

Stage 1
Stage 2
Stage 3

SUMMARIZE IT
Explain how intrusive rock features become visible above ground.

_____

_____

Tie It Together

Recently hired by the United States Geological Survey, you notice signs of activity coming from a large composite volcano and predict an eruption within the next few days. The volcano is near several small towns, and the people in these towns must be warned of the danger. On the lines below, prepare a broadcast to warn the townspeople of the eruption. Present your broadcast warning to the class. Include the following topics in your warning:

- Information about composite volcanoes

- The types of hazards that might occur

- What people should do to stay safe

_____

_____

_____

_____

_____

_____

_____

_____

_____

_____

_____

_____

_____

_____

_____

_____

Volcanoes Chapter Wrap-Up

Now that you have read the chapter, think about what you have learned and complete the table below. Compare your previous answers with these.

1. Write an **A** if you agree with the statement.
2. Write a **D** if you disagree with the statement.

Volcanoes	After You Read
• One volcano in Hawaii has been erupting for hundreds of years.	
• Lava is called magma when it reaches Earth's surface.	
• All volcanoes have the same type of eruptions.	
• Volcanic activity can form underground rock features.	

Review

Use this checklist to help you study.

☐ Review the information you included in your Foldable.

☐ Study your *Science Notebook* on this chapter.

☐ Study the definitions of vocabulary words.

☐ Review daily homework assignments.

☐ Re-read the chapter and review the charts, graphs, and illustrations.

☐ Review the Self Check at the end of each section.

☐ Look over the Chapter Review at the end of the chapter.

SUMMARIZE IT After reading this chapter, identify three things that you have learned about volcanoes.

_____

_____

_____

_____

Copyright © Glencoe/McGraw-Hill, a division of The McGraw-Hill Companies, Inc.

Clues to Earth's Past

Before You Read

Before you read the chapter, respond to these statements.

1. Write an **A** if you agree with the statement.
2. Write a **D** if you disagree with the statement.

Before You Read	Clues to Earth's Past
	• The footprint of a dinosaur is considered a fossil.
	• Scientists use fossils to learn what an environment was like long ago.
	• The oldest rock layer is always the one found on top.
	• Scientists can determine the age of some rocks.

 *Construct the Foldable as directed at the beginning of this chapter.*

Science Journal

List three fossils that you would expect to find a million years from now in the place you live today.

_____

_____

_____

_____

_____

Clues to Earth's Past
Section 1 Fossils

Skim *Section 1 of your book. Read the headings and examine the illustrations. Write three questions that come to mind.*

1. _____

2. _____

3. _____

Review Vocabulary **Define** paleontologist *to show its scientific meaning.*

paleontologist _____

_____

New Vocabulary *Define the following terms to show their scientific meaning.*

permineralized remains _____

_____

carbon film _____

_____

cast _____

_____

index fossils _____

_____

Academic Vocabulary *Define* emerge *to show its scientific meaning.*

emerge _____

_____

Section 1 Fossils (continued)

| **Main Idea** | **Details** |

Formation of Fossils

I found this information on page _____.

Complete *the table to describe the two conditions that improve the chances of fossil formation. Give an example of each.*

Condition	Example

Types of Preservation

I found this information on page _____.

Create *a concept web to summarize the types of preservation.*

I found this information on page _____.

Sequence *the steps involved in the making of the cast of a shell.*

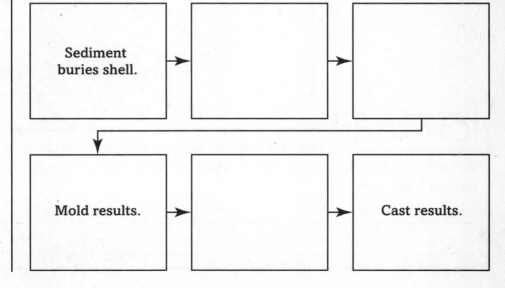

Sediment buries shell. → □ → □

Mold results. → □ → Cast results.

Section 1 Fossils (continued)

Main Idea ~ _____ ~ Details ~

Index Fossils

I found this information on page _____.

Summarize *the three characteristics of* index fossils.

1. _____

2. _____

3. _____

Analyze *why index fossils are more useful to paleontologists than many other fossils.*

_____

_____

_____

_____

Fossils and Ancient Environments

I found this information on page _____.

Organize *the kinds of information about ancient environments that scientists can learn from fossils. Complete the graphic organizer.*

Information about environment revealed by fossils

CONNECT IT

You find a fossil shell in a layer of rock. It appears to be a clam. What type of rock must the rock layer be? What type of environment would the animal have lived in?

_____

_____

Clues to Earth's Past
Section 2 Relative Ages of Rocks

Scan *the list below to preview Section 2 of your book.*

- Read all section headings.

- Read all bold words.

- Look at all of the pictures.

- Think about what you already know about rock.

Write three facts you discovered about the relative ages of rocks as you scanned the section.

1. _____

2. _____

3. _____

Review Vocabulary

Define sedimentary rock *to show its scientific meaning.*

sedimentary rock

_____

_____

New Vocabulary

Read each definition below. Write the correct vocabulary term in the blank to the left.

_____ states that in undisturbed rock layers, the oldest rocks are on the bottom and the rocks are progressively younger toward the top

_____ age of something compared with the ages of other things

_____ gap in a sequence of rock layers that is due to erosion or periods without any deposition

Academic Vocabulary

Define sequence *to show its scientific meaning.*

sequence

_____

_____

Section 2 Relative Ages of Rocks (continued)

Main Idea   **Details**

Superposition

I found this information on page _____.

Model *the principle of superposition by sketching a cross-section of layers of undisturbed sedimentary rock. Number the layers, starting with 1 for the oldest layer.*

Relative Ages

I found this information on page _____.

Describe *how the relative age of a rock layer is different from the actual age of the rock layer.*

_____

_____

_____

_____

_____

I found this information on page _____.

Model *how a folded rock formation containing limestone, coal, and sandstone would form. Draw and label the layers as they would form originally. Then draw what they would look like after being folded.*

Section 2 Relative Ages of Rocks (continued)

| Main Idea | Details |

Unconformities

I found this information on page _____.

Compare and contrast *angular unconformity, disconformity, and* nonconformity *in rocks by sequencing the steps in their formation.*

Unconformities	
Type	**How It Forms**
Angular unconformity	1. 2. 3.
Disconformity	1. 2. 3.
Nonconformity	1. 2. 3.

Matching Up Rock Layers

I found this information on page _____.

Identify *the two ways to match up, or correlate, exposed rock layers from two different places. Complete the graphic organizer.*

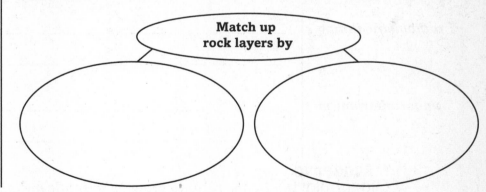

Match up rock layers by

SYNTHESIZE IT As you pass through a highway cut, you notice distinct layers of rock. Can you be sure that the top layer is the youngest one? Explain.

_____

_____

Clues to Earth's Past
Section 3 Absolute Ages of Rocks

Predict *three things that might be discussed in Section 3 as you read the headings.*

1. _____

_____

2. _____

_____

3. _____

_____

Review Vocabulary   **Define** isotopes *to show its scientific meaning.*

isotopes _____

_____

New Vocabulary   *Define these key terms to show their scientific meaning.*

radioactive decay _____

_____

radiometric dating _____

_____

uniformitarianism _____

_____

Academic Vocabulary   *Define ratio to show its scientific meaning.*

ratio _____

_____

Section 3 Absolute Ages of Rocks (continued)

Main Idea	Details

Absolute Ages and Radioactive Decay

I found this information on page _____.

Organize *information about radioactive decay as a tool to find a rock's absolute age. Complete the Venn diagram below with at least six points of information.*

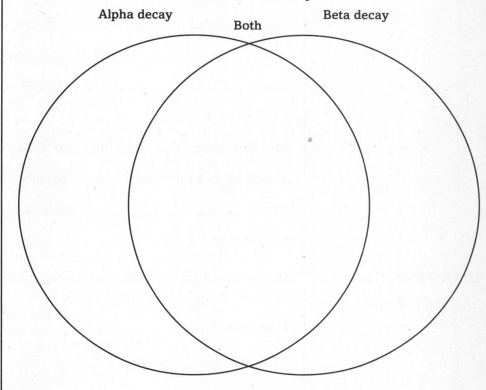

I found this information on page _____.

Create *a bar chart to show four half-lives. Then draw a curve connecting the tops of the bars. Label each axis.*

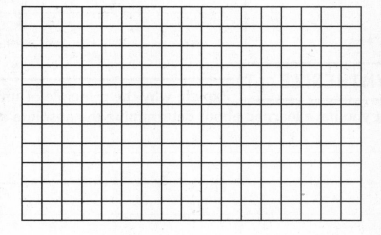

Half-lives

Section 3 Absolute Ages of Rocks (continued)

⟨ Main Idea ⟩ _____ **⟨ Details ⟩** _____

Radiometric Ages

I found this information on page _____.

Analyze *carbon-14 dating by completing the statements.*

The half-life of carbon-14 is _____.

When carbon-14 decays, it becomes _____.

Carbon-14 radiometric dating is used for _____,

_____, and _____ samples up

to _____ old. Scientists compare amounts of

carbon-14 in the _____ to the amount in a fossil

of an organism that lived long ago. While the organism was alive,

it took in and processed carbon-14 and _____.

The _____ of carbon-14 to carbon-12 tells the

approximate _____ of the fossil.

Uniformitarianism

I found this information on page _____.

Summarize *Hutton's view of uniformitarianism and the modern view of changes that affect Earth.*

Hutton's view: _____

_____

_____

Modern view: _____

_____

_____

⎡SYNTHESIZE IT⎤

Explain why the principle of uniformitarianism is critical to what you have learned about determining the absolute age of rocks.

_____

_____

_____

_____

Tie It Together

A paleontologist found the following composition of rock layers at a site. The paleontologist concludes that no folding or other disruption has happened to the layers. What can you conclude about the area's history? Write a summary of your conclusions.

Top layer: coal layer made up of altered plant material

Middle layer: mix of sandstone and shale, with some tracks made by dinosaurs

Bottom layer: limestone with fossils of clams, snails, and sea lilies

_____

_____

_____

_____

_____

_____

_____

_____

_____

_____

_____

_____

_____

_____

_____

_____

Clues to Earth's Past Chapter Wrap-Up

Now that you have read the chapter, think about what you have learned and complete the table below. Compare your previous answers with these.

1. Write an **A** if you agree with the statement.
2. Write a **D** if you disagree with the statement.

Clues to Earth's Past	After You Read
• The footprint of a dinosaur is considered a fossil.	
• Scientists use fossils to learn what an environment was like long ago.	
• The oldest rock layer is always the one found on top.	
• Scientists can determine the age of some rocks.	

Review

Use this checklist to help you study.

☐ Review the information you included in your Foldable.

☐ Study your *Science Notebook* on this chapter.

☐ Study the definitions of vocabulary words.

☐ Review daily homework assignments.

☐ Re-read the chapter and review the charts, graphs, and illustrations.

☐ Review the Self Check at the end of each section.

☐ Look over the Chapter Review at the end of the chapter.

SUMMARIZE IT

Identify three facts about fossils and rock layers that you found interesting.

_____

_____

_____

_____

Geologic Time

Before You Read

Preview the chapter title, section titles, and section headings. Complete the first two columns of the table by listing at least two ideas for each section in each column.

K What I know	W What I want to find out

Construct the Foldable as directed at the beginning of this chapter.

Science Journal

Describe how an animal or a plant might change if Earth becomes hotter in the next million years.

_____

_____

_____

_____

_____

Geologic Time
Section 1 Life and Geologic Time

Skim *the headings in Section 1. Predict two topics that will be covered in this section.*

1. _____

2. _____

Review Vocabulary

Define fossils *to show its scientific meaning.*

fossils | _____

New Vocabulary

Write the correct vocabulary term next to each definition.

_____ representation of Earth's history that shows the time units used to divide it

_____ longest subdivision of geologic time

_____ second-longest subdivision of geologic time

_____ subdivision of an era

_____ subdivision of a period

_____ change of species through time

_____ group of organisms that normally reproduce only with other members of their group

_____ process by which organisms that have characteristics that are better suited to an environment have a better chance of surviving and reproducing than those that do not

_____ organism with a three-lobed exoskeleton that was abundant in Paleozoic oceans

_____ large ancient landmass composed of all the continents joined together

Academic Vocabulary

Use a dictionary to define survive.

survive | _____

Name _____ **Date** _____

Section 1 Life and Geologic Time (continued)

Main Idea	Details

Geologic Time

I found this information on page _____ .

Distinguish *the units of geologic time. Give examples of each.*

Largest subdivision: _____

    Examples: _____

Second-largest subdivision: _____

    Examples: _____

Third-largest subdivision: _____

    Examples: _____

Fourth-largest subdivision: _____

    Examples: _____

Complete *the table to identify when each of the following key developments in the history of Earth occurred.*

Event	Eon	Era (if identified)	Period (if identified)
First life			
First trilobites			
First flowering plants			

Organic Evolution

I found this information on page _____ .

Sequence *the steps of* natural selection *as described by Darwin.*

1. _____

    _____

2. _____

    _____

3. _____

    _____

Section 1 Life and Geologic Time (continued)

Main Idea	Details

Main Idea

I found this information on page _____.

Identify *two factors that are necessary for natural selection to occur within a species.*

1. _____

2. _____

Trilobites

I found this information on page _____.

Organize *information about how trilobites evolved over time. Complete the flow charts.*

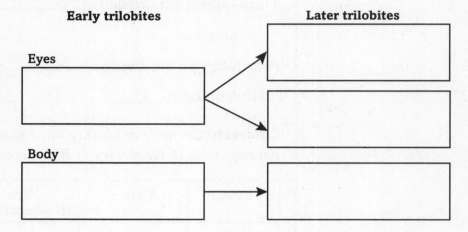

Early trilobites   Later trilobites

Eyes

Body

Plate Tectonics and Earth History

I found this information on page _____.

Contrast *two theories explaining the extinction of trilobites at the end of the Paleozoic era. Fill in the missing words.*

Some scientists believe that the formation of _____

caused _____ .

Trilobites could not _____ .

Other scientists suggest that _____

_____ caused the extinction.

CONNECT IT

Compare and contrast natural selection and artificial selection.

_____

_____

_____

_____

Geologic Time
Section 2 Early Earth History

Skim *Section 2. Write three questions that come to mind from looking at the headings and illustrations.*

1. _____

2. _____

3. _____

Review Vocabulary   **Define** life *to show its scientific meaning.*

life

_____

_____

New Vocabulary   *Use your book to define each vocabulary term.*

Precambrian time

_____

_____

cyanobacteria

_____

_____

Paleozoic Era

_____

_____

Academic Vocabulary   *Use a dictionary to define* hypothesis. *Use* hypothesis *in a sentence to show its scientific meaning.*

hypothesis

_____

_____

_____

_____

Section 2 Early Earth History (continued)

⬭ **Main Idea** ⬭   ⬭ **Details** ⬭

Precambrian Time

I found this information on page _____.

Summarize *two reasons why little is known about the organisms that lived during Precambrian time.*

1. _____

_____

2. _____

_____

I found this information on page _____.

Sequence *important events in the evolution of life during Precambrian time. Complete the flowchart.*

The first _____ appeared on Earth. They used

_____ and produced _____ .

⬇

⬇

The Paleozoic Era

I found this information on page _____.

Organize *information about life during the* Paleozoic Era. *Complete the concept web with examples of life that appeared during the Paleozoic Era.*

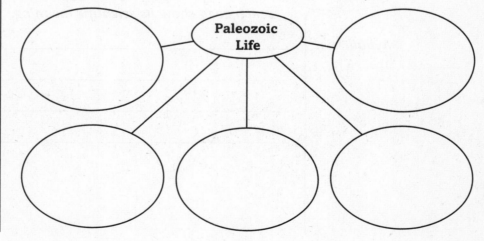

Section 2 **Early Earth History** (continued)

Main Idea	**Details**
The Paleozoic Era	**Analyze** *how the characteristics of amphibians and reptiles allowed them to live on land.*

I found this information on page _____.

Amphibians	
Characteristic	Effect
Lungs	
Legs	

Reptiles	
Characteristic	Effect
Protective coating on eggs	
Skin covered with hard scales	

I found this information on page _____.

Organize *information about three possible explanations of the extinctions that took place at the end of the Paleozoic Era.*

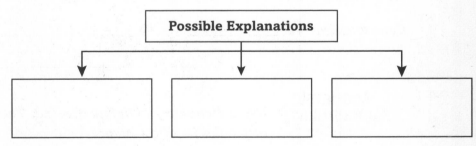

Possible Explanations

SYNTHESIZE IT Analyze why rock formations that show the soft parts of Paleozoic organisms are important.

_____

_____

_____

Geologic Time

Section 3 Middle and Recent Earth History

Preview *the* What You'll Learn *statements for Section 3. Rewrite each statement as a question. Look for the answers as you read.*

1. _____

_____

2. _____

_____

3. _____

_____

Review Vocabulary

Define dinosaur *to show its scientific meaning.*

dinosaur

_____

_____

New Vocabulary

Use your book to define each vocabulary term.

Mesozoic Era

_____

_____

Cenozoic Era

_____

_____

Academic Vocabulary

Use a dictionary to define diverse. *Then use the term in an original scientific sentence.*

diverse

_____

_____

_____

Section 3 Middle and Recent Earth History (continued)

Main Idea	Details

The Mesozoic Era

I found this information on page _____.

Organize *key information about dinosaurs.*

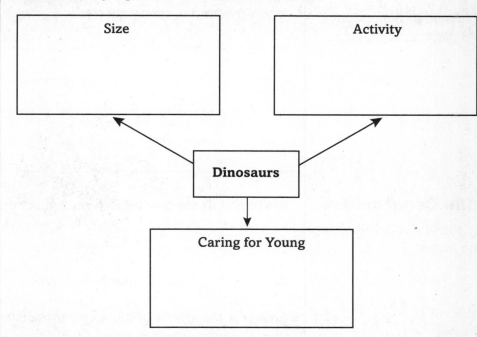

I found this information on page _____.

Complete *the chart to identify key characteristics of other important organisms from the* **Mesozoic Era.**

	Description	When They Appeared
Birds		
Mammals		
Gymnosperms		
Angiosperms		

Section 3 Middle and Recent Earth History (continued)

Main Idea	Details
The Mesozoic Era *I found this information on page _____.*	**Summarize** *what happened at the end of the Mesozoic Era to the environment and many species.* _____ _____ _____ _____ _____
The Cenozoic Era *I found this information on page _____.*	**Distinguish** *the two periods that make up the Cenozoic Era* 1. _____, began about _____ million years ago 2. _____, began about _____ million years ago **Analyze** *the effects of changes that occurred during the* Cenozoic Era. *Complete the diagrams.*

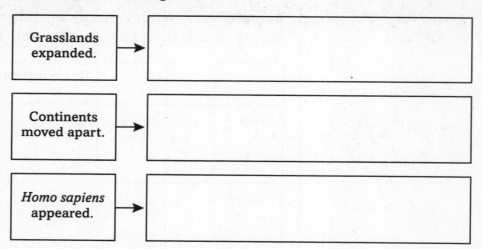

Grasslands expanded. →

Continents moved apart. →

Homo sapiens appeared. →

SYNTHESIZE IT

Infer how paleontologists study the behaviors of extinct animals, such as taking care of young.

_____

_____

_____

Tie It Together

You are directing a new movie about prehistoric times. The script you get shows humans interacting with dinosaurs. Write a memo to the scriptwriter explaining why this would not be scientifically accurate. Suggest two other possible settings, one that includes dinosaurs and one that includes humans.

Memo:

_____

_____

_____

_____

_____

_____

_____

_____

_____

_____

_____

_____

_____

_____

_____

_____

_____

Geologic Time Chapter Wrap-Up

After You Read

Review the ideas you listed in the chart at the beginning of the chapter. Cross out any incorrect information in the first column. Then complete the chart by filling in the third column.

K What I know	W What I want to find out	L What I learned

Review

Use this checklist to help you study.

☐ Review the information you included in your Foldable.

☐ Study your *Science Notebook* on this chapter.

☐ Study the definitions of vocabulary words.

☐ Review daily homework assignments.

☐ Re-read the chapter and review the charts, graphs, and illustrations.

☐ Review the Self Check at the end of each section.

☐ Look over the Chapter Review at the end of the chapter.

SUMMARIZE IT

After reading this chapter, identify three things that you have learned about geologic time.

_____

_____

_____

_____

Atmosphere

Before You Read

Before you read the chapter, respond to these statements.

1. Write an **A** if you agree with the statement.
2. Write a **D** if you disagree with the statement.

Before You Read	Atmosphere
	• Earth's early atmosphere was produced by erupting volcanoes.
	• Nitrogen makes up most of Earth's atmosphere.
	• Energy from the Moon causes winds and ocean currents.
	• Wind is the movement of air from an area of higher pressure to an area of lower pressure.

 *Construct the Foldable as directed at the beginning of this chapter.*

Science Journal

Write an article describing how you might prepare to climb Mt. Everest.

_____

_____

_____

_____

_____

_____

_____

Atmosphere
Section 1 Earth's Atmosphere

Skim *the headings in Section 1. Then make three predictions about what you will learn.*

1. _____

_____

2. _____

_____

3. _____

_____

Review Vocabulary

Define pressure *in a sentence that shows its scientific meaning.*

pressure _____

New Vocabulary

Use your book or a dictionary to define the following key terms.

atmosphere _____

_____

ionosphere _____

_____

ultraviolet radiation _____

_____

chlorofluorocarbon _____

_____

Academic Vocabulary

Use a dictionary to define trace *in terms of a scientific amount.*

trace _____

_____

Section 1 Earth's Atmosphere (continued)

Main Idea	Details

Importance of the Atmosphere

I found this information on page _____.

Summarize *why Earth's atmosphere is important to life on Earth.*

_____

_____

_____

Makeup of the Atmosphere

I found this information on page _____.

Compare *the amount of gases in the atmosphere by rereading the section and analyzing the circle graph in your book. Then complete the following paragraph.*

The gas that makes up most of the atmosphere is _____.

_____ makes up 21 percent of the atmosphere. Oxygen

gas is important because _____

_____ Although carbon dioxide

makes up only 0.03% of the atmosphere it is a concern because

_____

_____

Layers of the Atmosphere

I found this information on page _____.

Model *the layers of the atmosphere by drawing them. Label and describe the characteristics of each layer.*

Section 1 Earth's Atmosphere (continued)

Main Idea | Details

Atmospheric Pressure

I found this information on page _____.

Model *how* air pressure *changes as you go higher in the atmosphere by creating a drawing in which dots represent air molecules. To the right, describe the cause of air pressure.*

Air Molecules

_____

_____

_____

_____

_____

_____

Temperature in Atmospheric Layers

I found this information on page _____.

Compare *the temperature changes that occur as you go higher in the troposphere, stratosphere, mesosphere, and thermosphere. Use the figure in your book to help you.*

_____

_____

_____

_____

_____

_____

_____

_____

CONNECT IT Why did many governments around the world agree to ban the production and use of CFCs in the mid-1990s?

_____

_____

_____

Atmosphere

Section 2 Energy Transfer in the Atmosphere

Skim *through Section 2 of your book. Write three questions that come to mind from reading the headings and examining the illustrations.*

1. _____

2. _____

3. _____

Use your book to define the term evaporation.

evaporation

_____

_____

New Vocabulary *Write the correct key term next to each definition.*

_____ energy that is transferred in the form of rays or waves

_____ transfer of energy that occurs when molecules bump into one another

_____ transfer of heat by the flow of material

_____ term that describes all of the water on Earth's surface

_____ process of water vapor changing to a liquid

Academic Vocabulary *Use a dictionary to define* transfer.

transfer

_____

_____

Section 2 Energy Transfer in the Atmosphere (continued)

Main Idea	Details

Energy from the Sun

I found this information on page _____.

Analyze *the figure in your book that shows what percent of the Sun's energy is absorbed and reflected by Earth. Then, label the circle graph to represent the data.*

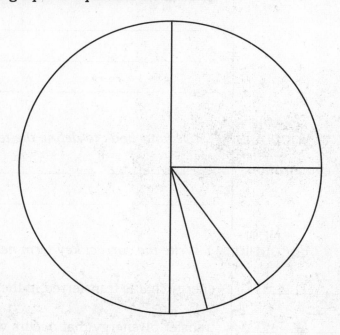

Heat

I found this information on page _____.

Compare and contrast *the three forms of energy transfer in the chart.*

Heat Energy	
Process	How Energy Is Transferred
Radiation	
Conduction	
Convection	

Describe *the types of energy transfer that occur when you burn your bare feet when walking on hot sand.*

_____

_____

Section 2 Energy Transfer in the Atmosphere (continued)

Main Idea	Details

The Water Cycle

I found this information on page _____.

Create *a flow chart to describe the water cycle.*

Earth's Atmosphere is Unique

I found this information on page _____.

Compare *Earth's atmosphere to the atmospheres of Venus and Mars.*

Amount of Heat Held by Atmospheres	
Planet	Description of Atmosphere
Venus	
Mars	
Earth	

SUMMARIZE IT

Infer from your reading three ways in which the atmosphere allows for life on Earth.

_____

_____

_____

_____

_____

Atmosphere
Section 3 Air Movement

Scan *Section 3 in your book. Then write three ways that moving air affects people.*

1. _____

2. _____

3. _____

Review Vocabulary *Use* density *in a sentence that shows its scientific meaning.*

density

_____

_____

New Vocabulary *Use the following key terms in a sentence that reflects its scientific meaning.*

Coriolis effect

_____

_____

jet stream

_____

_____

sea breeze

_____

_____

land breeze

_____

Academic Vocabulary *Use a dictionary to define* create.

create

_____

_____

Section 3 Air Movement (continued)

Main Idea	Details

Forming Wind

I found this information on page _____.

Sequence *how heated air and the Coriolis effect form wind.*

1.	The equator receives _____ _____
2.	As a result, air near the equator is _____ _____
3.	Dense air moves from _____ _____
4.	The rotation of Earth causes _____ _____
5.	Thus, the Coriolis effect causes _____ _____

Global Winds

I found this information on page _____.

Analyze *the models of the surface winds and winds of the upper troposphere in your book. Then complete the following statements.*

1. The equatorial doldrums are located at _____ latitude.

2. _____ blow from the east in areas north and south of the equator.

3. _____ move weather systems across most of North America.

4. Most surface wind systems are named _____ _____.

5. The jet stream in the United States travels from _____ _____.

6. The jet stream travels at the border between _____ _____.

Section 3 Air Movement (continued)

Main Idea

Details

Local Wind Systems

I found this information on page _____ .

Model *how air flows where the land meets the sea during the day and at night. Draw the two conditions below using arrows to indicate the direction of air flow.*

Day	Night

I found this information on page _____ .

Sequence *three steps that occurred in each of your drawings above.*

Day:	Night:
1.	1.
2.	2.
3.	3.

CONNECT IT Describe the role that the Sun's energy has in creating wind.

_____

_____

_____

Tie It Together

Model

Design a way to model how the curved surface of Earth affects how much direct sunlight the equator receives compared to the north pole. Discuss how you could test your model, and describe what you would hope to observe.

Materials might include: flashlight or lamp, a round object like a basketball, darkened room

1. _____

   _____

2. _____

   _____

Results: _____

_____

Atmosphere   Chapter Wrap-Up

Now that you have read the chapter, think about what you have learned and complete the table below. Compare your previous answers with these.

1. Write an **A** if you agree with the statement.
2. Write a **D** if you disagree with the statement.

Atmosphere	After You Read
• Earth's early atmosphere was produced by erupting volcanoes.	
• Nitrogen makes up most of Earth's atmosphere.	
• Energy from the Moon causes winds and ocean currents.	
• Wind is the movement of air from an area of higher pressure to an area of lower pressure.	

Review

Use this checklist to help you study.

☐ Review the information you included in your Foldable.

☐ Study your *Science Notebook* on this chapter.

☐ Study the definitions of vocabulary words.

☐ Review daily homework assignments.

☐ Re-read the chapter and review the charts, graphs, and illustrations.

☐ Review the Self Check at the end of each section.

☐ Look over the Chapter Review at the end of the chapter.

SUMMARIZE IT

After reading this chapter, identify three things that you have learned about Earth's atmosphere.

_____

_____

_____

_____

Name _____ **Date** _____

Weather

Before You Read

Before you read the chapter, look at the headings throughout the chapter and complete the chart below.

What I know	What I want to find out

Construct the Foldable as directed at the beginning of this chapter.

Science Journal

Write three questions you would ask a meteorologist about weather.

_____

_____

_____

_____

_____

_____

Weather
Section 1 What is weather?

Scan *the headings of the paragraphs throughout Section 1.*
Write a sentence about a topic that interests you.

_____

_____

Review Vocabulary **Define** *each vocabulary word below.*

factor _____

New Vocabulary

weather _____

_____

humidity _____

_____

relative humidity _____

_____

dew point _____

_____

fog _____

_____

precipitation _____

_____

Academic Vocabulary *Use a dictionary to write a definition of* role.

role _____

_____

Name _____   **Date** _____

Section 1 **What is weather?** (continued)

Main Idea	**Details**

Weather Factors

I found this information on page _____ .

Organize *information about factors that determine the weather by completing the concept map.*

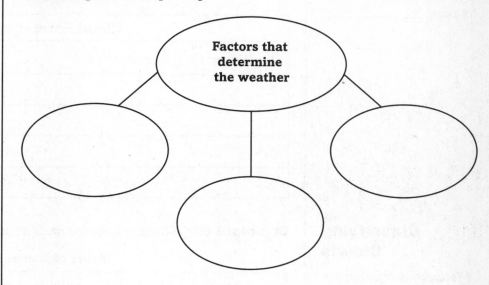

I found this information on page _____ .

Contrast *the characteristics of low and high air pressure.*

Air Pressure	
Low	High

Dew Point

I found this information on page _____ .

Summarize *the relationship between the* dew point *and the amount of water vapor in the air.*

_____

_____

_____

_____

Section 1 What is weather? (continued)

Main Idea ——————— **Details** ———————

Forming Clouds

I found this information on page _____.

Sequence *the steps in* cloud formation. *The first step is filled in for you.*

Cloud Formation	
1.	Warm air is forced upward.
2.	
3.	
4.	
5.	

Classifying Clouds

I found this information on page _____.

Complete *the following concept map about clouds and cloud types.*

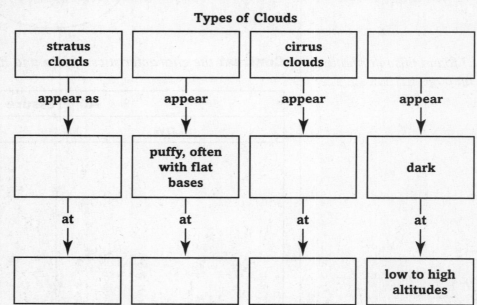

Types of Clouds

stratus clouds		cirrus clouds	
appear as	appear	appear	appear
	puffy, often with flat bases		dark
at	at	at	at
			low to high altitudes

CONNECT IT   A bottle of water sitting on a picnic table has droplets of water covering it. Analyze what this tells you about the temperatures of the water bottle and the air around it.

_____

_____

Weather
Section 2 Weather Patterns

Scan *the headings throughout Section 2. Write three questions about the topics covered in the section.*

1. _____

2. _____

3. _____

Review Vocabulary

Define barometer *using your book or a dictionary.*

barometer

_____

_____

New Vocabulary

Use your book or a dictionary to define each key term.

air mass

_____

_____

front

_____

_____

tornado

_____

_____

hurricane

_____

_____

blizzard

_____

Academic Vocabulary

Use a dictionary to define the term accompany.

accompany

_____

_____

Section 2 Weather Patterns (continued)

Main Idea

Details

Weather Changes

I found this information on page _____.

Classify *the characteristics of* air masses *according to where they develop by completing the table below.*

	Tropics	Polar regions
Land	warm, dry	
Water		

I found this information on page _____.

Model *the directions in which winds blow in high- and low-pressure systems of the northern hemisphere. Use arrows to draw the direction the winds move. Then describe the weather associated with each.*

Low-pressure Winds	High-pressure Winds

Fronts

I found this information on page _____.

Compare *and describe the four types of* fronts.

Fronts	
Type	Description

Section 2 Weather Patterns (continued)

Main Idea	Details

Severe Weather

I found this information on page _____.

Organize *the information on severe weather by completing the Venn diagram using the list of items below.*

- may be accompanied by damaging hail
- pose danger to people, structures, and animals
- measured by the Fujita scale
- the most powerful type of storm

- occurs in warm, moist air masses along fronts
- violently rotating column of air in contact with ground
- heavy rains can cause flooding
- turns heat from ocean into wind

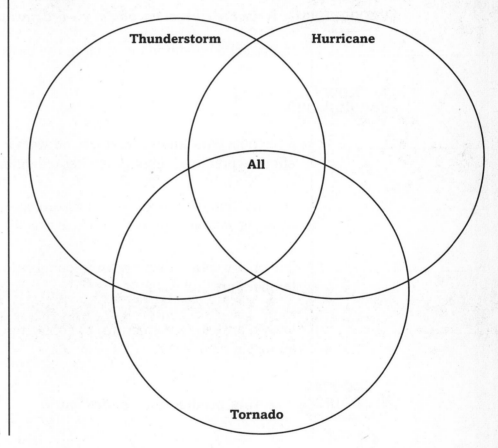

CONNECT IT   Summarize what actions to take during severe weather.

_____

_____

_____

Weather

Section 3 Weather Forecasts

Scan *the headings and look at the illustrations throughout Section 3.*
List four things you would like to learn about.

1. _____

2. _____

3. _____

4. _____

Review Vocabulary *Write the correct vocabulary word next to each definition.*

_____ | to predict a condition or event on the basis of observations

New Vocabulary

_____ | a scientist who studies weather and weather patterns in an effort to predict changing weather conditions

_____ | combination of symbols that meteorologists record on a map showing weather conditions at one specific location

_____ | line on a weather map drawn to connect locations of equal temperature

_____ | line on a weather map drawn to connect points of equal atmospheric pressure

Academic Vocabulary **Define** predict *using a dictionary.*

predict _____

_____

Section 3 Weather Forecasts (continued)

Main Idea

Details

Weather Observations

I found this information on page _____.

Organize *information about a meteorologist's work. List five measurements that a* meteorologist *takes and four instruments that improve a meteorologist's ability to predict weather.*

Measurements

1. _____

2. _____

3. _____

4. _____

5. _____

Instruments

1. _____

2. _____

3. _____

4. _____

Forecasting Weather

I found this information on page _____.

Compare and contrast isobars *and* isotherms *by completing the Venn diagram. List at least one descriptor in each part of the diagram.*

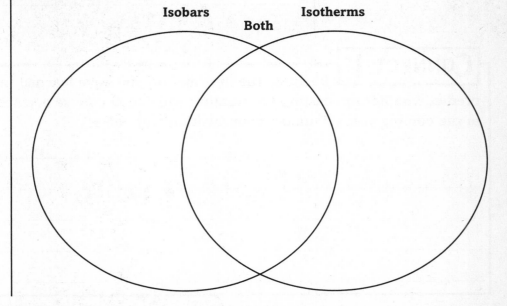

Isobars   Both   Isotherms

Section 3 Weather Forecasts (continued)

| Main Idea | Details |

Forecasting Weather

I found this information on page _____ .

Summarize *information provided by the spacing of isobars on a weather map by completing the chart.*

Spacing of Isobars		
	What spacing indicates about atmospheric pressure	What spacing indicates about wind conditions
Isobars close together		
Isobars far apart		

I found this information on page _____ .

Analyze *the information provided by the weather map in your book. Choose a city, and describe the weather it is experiencing.*

_____

_____

_____

_____

CONNECT IT Evaluate the information you have learned in this chapter to predict whether forecasting the weather will become more accurate or less accurate in the coming years. Support your position with facts.

_____

_____

_____

_____

_____

Tie It Together

Synthesize

You live in a region that sometimes is struck by hurricanes. Describe the plans that you would make to prepare for and respond to a hurricane.

Long-term planning for hurricane _____

_____

_____

_____

_____

_____

_____

When a hurricane has been predicted _____

_____

_____

_____

_____

_____

_____

Following a hurricane _____

_____

_____

_____

_____

_____

Weather   Chapter Wrap-Up

Review the chart that you completed before you read the chapter. Then complete the chart below.

What I learned	What I still want to find out

Review

Use this checklist to help you study.

- ☐ Review the information you included in your Foldable.
- ☐ Study your *Science Notebook* on this chapter.
- ☐ Study the definitions of vocabulary words.
- ☐ Review daily homework assignments.
- ☐ Re-read the chapter and review the charts, graphs, and illustrations.
- ☐ Review the Self Check at the end of each section.
- ☐ Look over the Chapter Review at the end of the chapter.

SUMMARIZE IT
After reading this chapter, identify three things that you have learned about weather.

_____

_____

_____

_____

_____

Climate

Before You Read

Before you read the chapter, respond to these statements.

1. Write an **A** if you agree with the statement.
2. Write a **D** if you disagree with the statement.

Before You Read	Climate
	• Climate is the state of the atmosphere at a specific time and place.
	• The polar zones generally have cooler temperatures because solar radiation hits these zones at a more direct angle.
	• The climate of an area can be affected by a large lake.
	• El Niño and La Niña are climatic events that can disrupt normal temperature and precipitation patterns around the world.

 *Construct the Foldable as directed at the beginning of this chapter.*

Science Journal

Write a paragraph explaining what you already know about the causes of seasons.

_____

_____

_____

_____

_____

_____

Climate

Section 1 What is climate?

Scan *the Section 1 headings and illustrations. Formulate two questions about this section that come to mind.*

1. _____

   _____

2. _____

   _____

Review Vocabulary **Define** *the following key terms to show their scientific meanings.*

latitude _____

_____

New Vocabulary

climate _____

_____

tropics _____

_____

polar zone _____

_____

temperate zone _____

_____

Academic Vocabulary

affect _____

_____

Copyright © Glencoe/McGraw-Hill, a division of The McGraw-Hill Companies, Inc.

Section 1 What is climate? (continued)

◀Main Idea▶   ◀Details▶

Latitude and Climate

I found this information on page _____.

Identify *and label the* climate zones *on the globe below. Also* include:

the equator   Tropic of Cancer   Tropic of Capricorn

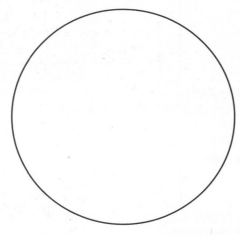

Other Factors

I found this information on page _____.

Organize *factors that affect climate on the concept map below.*

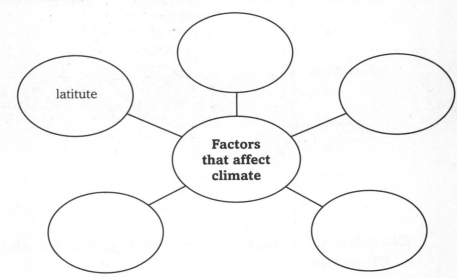

latitute

Factors that affect climate

COMPARE IT Contrast the climate of Buffalo, New York and Yuma, Arizona.
Discuss the geographical features that affect the two climates.

_____

_____

_____

Climate

Section 2 Climate Types

Predict *Read the title and the headings of Section 2. List three things that might be discussed in this section.*

1. _____

2. _____

3. _____

Review Vocabulary

Define *the following key terms. Use your book or a dictionary to help you.*

regions _____

_____

New Vocabulary

adaptation _____

_____

hibernation _____

_____

Academic Vocabulary

vary _____

_____

Classifying Climates

I found this information on page _____.

Complete *the following paragraph about climates.*

Wladimir Köppen developed a _____

_____. He noticed that different types of _____

_____. He was able to relate _____

_____ .

Section 2 Climate Types (continued)

Main Idea

Classifying Climates

I found this information on page _____.

Details

Summarize *the six major climate zones shown in your book. Describe the important characteristics of each.*

World Climates	
Climate Zone	**Description**

SYNTHESIZE IT Analyze the two types of adaptations organisms have to climate. Discuss structural and behavioral adaptations, give an example of each, and then tell how both are similar.

_____

_____

_____

_____

Climate

Section 3 Climate Changes

Scan *Use the checklist below to preview Section 3 of your book.*

☐ Read all section titles.

☐ Read all bold words.

☐ Look at all pictures, charts, and graphs.

☐ Think about what you already know about climates.

Write three facts you discovered about climatic changes as you scanned the section.

1. _____

2. _____

3. _____

Review Vocabulary **Define** solar radiation *using a dictionary.*

solar radiation _____

_____

New Vocabulary *Write the correct vocabulary term next to each definition.*

_____ increase in the average world temperature of Earth

_____ natural heating that occurs when certain gases in Earth's atmosphere trap heat

_____ climatic event that may occur when trade winds weaken or reverse, and can disrupt normal temperature and precipitation patterns around the world

_____ destruction of woodlands that can result in increased atmospheric carbon dioxide levels

_____ short period of climatic change caused by the tilt of Earth's axis as Earth revolves around the Sun

Academic Vocabulary *Use a dictionary to find the scientific definition of* reverse.

reverse _____

Section 3 Climate Changes (continued)

⬭ Main Idea ⬮	⬭ Details ⬮

Earth's Seasons

I found this information on page _____ .

Synthesize *information from your book to explain why the northern hemisphere has winter at the time when Earth is closest to the Sun.*

_____

_____

_____

_____

_____

_____

_____

El Niño and La Niña

I found this information on page _____ .

Contrast *conditions that occur during* El Niño *years with those that occur during* La Niña *years in the chart below.*

El Niño and La Niña		
	El Niño Year	La Niña Year
Strength of trade winds		
Water temperature along west coast of South America		
Typical climate effects		

Section 3 Climate Changes (continued)

Main Idea	Details
Climatic Change *I found this information on page* _____.	**Complete** *the paragraph below about* climate change.

In the past, Earth's overall climate has been _____

_____ and _____. During

the last two million years, Earth's climate has cycled between

_____ when glaciers advanced and _____

_____ when climate was similar to today's climate.

What causes climatic change?

I found this information on page _____.

Sequence *events to explain how an erupting volcano can cause short-term climate change.*

A volcano erupts adding small particles called aerosols to atmosphere.	→	

The particles block some sunlight from reaching Earth.	→	

Complete *the following chart about sunspots.*

Sunspots	
Definition of sunspots	How sunspots affect climate
Period between 1645 and 1715	Safety warning

Section 3 Climate Changes (continued)

<table>
<tr><td>Main Idea</td><td>Details</td></tr>
</table>

Climatic Changes Today

I found this information on page _____ .

Sequence *steps explaining the* greenhouse effect. *The first one has been done for you.*

The Greenhouse Effect	
1.	Radiation from the Sun strikes Earth's surface.
2.	
3.	
4.	
5.	

Global Warming and Human Activities and The Carbon Cycle

I found this information on page _____ .

Analyze global warming *by completing the concept map below.*

Definition _____

_____

Global Warming

Related Human Activities	Effect on carbon cycle

SYNTHESIZE IT Analyze how humans impact Earth's atmosphere and how it may have long term effects on global climates.

_____

_____

_____

Climate Chapter Wrap-Up

Now that you have read the chapter, think about what you have learned and complete the table below. Compare your previous answers with these.

    1. Write an **A** if you agree with the statement.

    2. Write a **D** if you disagree with the statement.

Climate	After You Read
• Climate is the state of the atmosphere at a specific time and place.	
• The polar zones generally have cooler temperatures because solar radiation hits these zones at a more direct angle.	
• The climate of an area can be affected by a large lake.	
• El Niño and La Niña are climatic events that can disrupt normal temperature and precipitation patterns around the world.	

Review

Use this checklist to help you study.

☐ Review the information you included in your Foldable.

☐ Study your *Science Notebook* on this chapter.

☐ Study the definitions of vocabulary words.

☐ Review daily homework assignments.

☐ Re-read the chapter and review the charts, graphs, and illustrations.

☐ Review the Self Check at the end of each section.

☐ Look over the Chapter Review at the end of the chapter.

SUMMARIZE IT   After reading this chapter, identify three things that you have learned about climate.

_____

_____

_____

_____

Ocean Motion

Before You Read

Preview the chapter title, the section titles, and the section headings. List at least one idea for each section in each column.

K What I know	W What I want to find out

 *Construct the Foldable as directed at the beginning of this chapter.*

Science Journal

Record some facts you know about ocean currents, waves, or tides. Include some pictures to show your ideas.

_____

_____

_____

_____

_____

_____

_____

Ocean Motion
Section 1 Ocean Water

Scan *the headings in Section 1 of your book. Predict three topics that will be discussed.*

1. _____

2. _____

3. _____

Review Vocabulary

Define resource *using your book or a dictionary.*

resource

_____

_____

New Vocabulary

Use your book or a dictionary to define the vocabulary terms. Then use each term in a sentence that shows its scientific meaning.

basin

_____

_____

_____

_____

salinity

_____

_____

_____

_____

Academic Vocabulary

Use a dictionary to define constant *to show its scientific meaning.*

constant

_____

_____

Name _____ **Date** _____

Section 1 Ocean Water (continued)

Main Idea

Details

Importance of Oceans and **Origin of Oceans**

_I found this information on page _____._

Organize _information about the_ importance of oceans _by completing the chart below._

Importance of Oceans	
Type of Use	**Examples**
Food	
Energy	
Minerals	
Transportation	

Model _the_ part of Earth that is covered by oceans _by shading in the correct percentage in the blocks below. Each block is equal to ten percent._

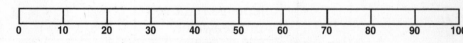

0   10   20   30   40   50   60   70   80   90   100

Percentage of Earth Covered by Oceans

Composition of Oceans

_I found this information on page _____._

Summarize _the_ composition of ocean water _by completing the graphic organizer._

Ocean Water contains

dissolved _____	dissolved salts
Examples: _____, nitrogen, and _____	**Examples:** _____, _____, sulfate, _____, potassium, and _____
Sources: the _____, respiration, and _____	**Sources:** _____ from dissolved _____ carried by rivers and erupting _____

Section 1 Ocean Water (continued)

Main Idea _____ **Details**

I found this information on page _____.

Complete *the statement about* how minerals form in seawater.

As seawater _____, ions, such as _____ and sodium, _____ to form minerals called _____.

I found this information on page _____.

Organize *information about* salinity *in the chart below.*

Salinity	
Definition	
How is it measured?	
How are elements added to seawater?	
How are dissolved elements removed from seawater?	

I found this information on page _____.

Create *an organizer to list three ways people can* remove salt from ocean water.

SUMMARIZE IT How does a solar desalination plant make use of natural processes of the water cycle and gravity to remove salts and produce freshwater?

_____

_____

_____

Name _____   Date _____

Ocean Motion
Section 2 Ocean Currents

Skim *Section 2 of your book. Write three questions that come to mind. Look for answers to your questions as you read the section.*

1. _____

2. _____

3. _____

Review Vocabulary

circulation

Define circulation *using your book or a dictionary.*

_____

_____

New Vocabulary

Read the definitions below. Write the correct vocabulary term on the blank to the left of each definition.

_____   forms when a mass of more dense seawater sinks beneath less dense seawater

_____   causes moving air and water to turn left in the southern hemisphere and turn right in the northern hemisphere due to Earth's rotation

_____   wind-powered ocean current that moves the upper few hundred meters of seawater horizontally, parallel to Earth's surface

_____   vertical circulation in the ocean that brings deep, cold water to the ocean surface

Academic Vocabulary

layer

Use a dictionary to define layer. *Then use the term in a sentence to show its scientific meaning.*

_____

_____

_____

Section 2 Ocean Currents (continued)

Main Idea ——————————— **Details** —————

Surface Currents

I found this information on page _____.

Describe *the characteristics of* surface currents *by completing the graphic organizer below.*

```
┌─────────────────┐        ┌──────────┐        ┌─────────────────┐
│ Parallel to     │ ─────▶ │ Surface  │ ◀───── │ Turned by the   │
│                 │        │ Currents │        │                 │
│ _____ │        └──────────┘        │ _____ │
└─────────────────┘      ▲     ▲     ▲          └─────────────────┘
┌─────────────────┐    ┌─────────────┐        ┌─────────────────┐
│ Powered by      │    │ Move in huge,│        │ Move only the upper│
│                 │    │             │        │                 │
│ _____ │    │ _____ │        │ _____ │
│                 │    │             │        │                 │
│ _____ │    │ patterns    │        │ meters of seawater│
└─────────────────┘    └─────────────┘        └─────────────────┘
```

I found this information on page _____.

Complete *the sequence to explain how* surface currents form.

1. Surface _____ cause water to _____ in the ocean.

2. _____ pulls water off the pile.

3. The Coriolis effect _____ the water.

4. The surface water _____ around the piles of water.

I found this information on page _____.

Model *the direction that* surface currents circulate *for the areas of Earth listed in the chart by drawing arrows showing the direction of the currents.*

Surface Currents	
Place on Earth	**Direction of Current**
North of the equator	
South of the equator	

Section 2 Ocean Currents (continued)

Main Idea	Details

Main Idea

I found this information on page _____.

Details

Analyze *how* surface currents affect climate *by completing the flow chart below.*

_____ surface currents flow _____ from the equator.	_____ is released.
	The _____ is warmed.

Upwelling

I found this information on page _____.

Summarize *an effect of* upwelling.

_____

_____

Density Currents

I found this information on page _____.

Compare *information about* density currents *as they form in the Antarctic and the North Atlantic oceans.*

Density Currents		
Where does it form?	Antarctic	North Atlantic
How does it form?		
Where does it move?		

SUMMARIZE IT

Compare the characteristics of surface currents with those of density currents.

_____

_____

Ocean Motion
Section 3 Ocean Waves and Tides

Scan *the* What You'll Learn *statements for Section 3 of your book. Identify three topics that will be discussed.*

1. _____

2. _____

3. _____

Review Vocabulary

Define energy *using your book or a dictionary.*

energy _____

New Vocabulary

Write a paragraph using the three vocabulary terms.

wave
crest
trough

_____

_____

_____

_____

_____

Read the definitions below. Write the correct vocabulary term on the blank to the left of each definition.

_____   collapsing ocean wave that forms in shallow water and breaks onto the shore

_____   difference between the level of the ocean at high tide and the level at low tide

_____   daily rise and fall of sea level caused by the gravitational pull of the Sun and the Moon on Earth

Academic Vocabulary

Use a dictionary to define range *to show its meaning in science and math.*

range _____

_____

Section 3 Ocean Waves and Tides (continued)

Main Idea	Details

Waves

I found this information on page _____.

Model *a wave below by drawing it and labeling the following parts:* crest, trough, wavelength, *and* wave height.

I found this information on page _____.

Summarize *information in your book to complete the chart about waves.*

Waves	
Question	Answer
How do waves form?	
How does water move in waves?	
What do waves carry?	
When do waves stop forming?	
What affects the height of waves?	

I found this information on page _____.

Sequence *the formation of a* breaker *onto shore.*

1. _____ slows water at the bottom of a wave near shore.

2. The _____ of the wave keeps _____.

3. The top of the wave outruns the bottom and _____,

   or _____, onto the shore.

4. _____ pulls the water back to sea.

Name _____ Date _____

Section 3 Ocean Waves and Tides (continued)

Main Idea   **Details**

Tides

I found this information on page _____.

Complete *the graphic organizer about* tides.

```
                    ┌──────────────┐
                    │    Tides     │
                    └──────────────┘
                           │
                           ▼
```

Are _____ produced by the _____

_____ .

```
                           │
                           ▼
```

Each giant wave is usually 1 to 2 _____ high. Its _____
is thousands of kilometers long.

```
             │                              │
             ▼                              ▼
```

High Tide	**Low Tide**
As the *crest* nears shore, the sea seems to _____ .	As the *trough* nears shore, the sea seems to _____ .

```
             │                              │
             ▼                              ▼
```

The _____ between the level of the ocean at high tide

and the level at low tide is _____ .

CONNECT IT Draw two pictures, one that shows waves forming in wind that
is blowing at 5 kilometers per hour and one that shows waves forming in wind that is
blowing at 20 kilometers per hour. Describe how the waves in each picture are different.

```
┌─────────────────────────┐   ┌─────────────────────────┐
│                         │   │                         │
│                         │   │                         │
│                         │   │                         │
│                         │   │                         │
└─────────────────────────┘   └─────────────────────────┘
```

_____

_____

Copyright © Glencoe/McGraw-Hill, a division of The McGraw-Hill Companies, Inc.

Tie It Together

Tracking Currents

Goods lost from wrecked ships have been used to track ocean currents. Read about tracking ocean currents in your book. Then, using the map of surface currents in your book, predict where 80,000 pairs of shoes lost overboard by a freighter in the northern Pacific would wash ashore. Explain your prediction, and draw a picture showing the paths the shoes might travel.

Prediction: _____

_____

_____

_____

Ocean Motion   Chapter Wrap-Up

Review the ideas you listed in the chart at the beginning of the chapter. Cross out any incorrect information in the first column. Then complete the chart by filling in the third column.

K What I know	W What I want to find out	L What I learned

Review

Use this checklist to help you study.

- ☐ Review the information you included in your Foldable.
- ☐ Study your *Science Notebook* on this chapter.
- ☐ Study the definitions of vocabulary words.
- ☐ Review daily homework assignments.
- ☐ Re-read the chapter and review the charts, graphs, and illustrations.
- ☐ Review the Self Check at the end of each section.
- ☐ Look over the Chapter Review at the end of the chapter.

SUMMARIZE IT
After reading this chapter, identify three main ideas from the chapter.

_____

_____

_____

_____

Oceanography

Before You Read

Before you read the chapter, respond to these statements.

1. Write an **A** if you agree with the statement.
2. Write a **D** if you disagree with the statement.

Before You Read	Oceanography
	• Sediment that originates on land rarely settles as far as the deep ocean floor.
	• Hot water streams out into surrounding seawater through holes and cracks along mid-ocean ridges.
	• The Sun is the source of nearly all of the energy used by organisms in the ocean.
	• Factories sometimes release chemicals into streams that eventually empty into the ocean.

 *Construct the Foldable as directed at the beginning of this chapter.*

Science Journal

Describe characteristics of three marine organisms you are familiar with.

_____

_____

_____

_____

Oceanography
Section 1 The Seafloor

Predict *three things that might be discussed as you scan the headings and illustrations of Section 1.*

1. _____

2. _____

3. _____

Review Vocabulary

magma

Define magma *using its scientific meaning.*

_____

_____

New Vocabulary

abyssal plain

mid-ocean ridge

trench

Use your book to define the following terms.

_____

_____

_____

_____

_____

_____

Academic Vocabulary

locate

Use a dictionary to find the scientific definition of **locate.**

_____

_____

Section 1 The Seafloor (continued)

Main Idea

The Ocean Basins

I found this information on page _____.

Details

Model *the ocean basin. Label each of the following features in your drawing.*

- ab____al plain
- co____ntal shelf
- continental slope
- where new ocean crust forms
- where ocean crust is destroyed

- oceanic trench
- seamount
- volcanic island
- mid-ocean ridge

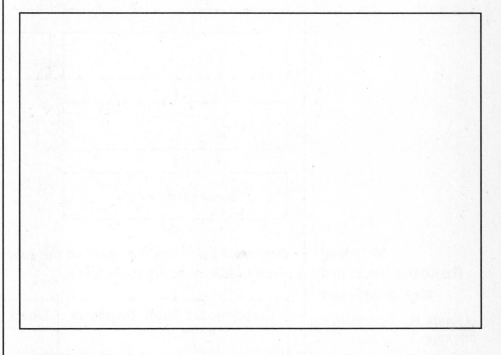

Distinguish *between the* continental shelf *and the* continental slope *by inserting one fact into each section of the Venn diagram.*

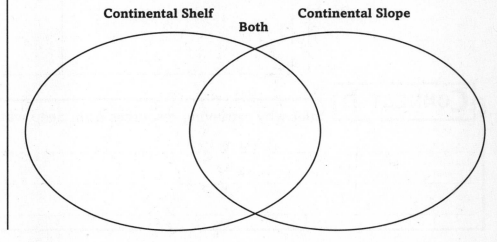

Main Idea

Details

Ridges and Trenches

I found this information on page _____.

Sequence *how seafloor is constantly forming and being destroyed.*

At Mid-Ocean Ridges	At Subduction Zones
↓	↓
↓	↓
	seafloor is destroyed
↓	
↓	
new ocean floor forms	

Mineral Resources from the Seafloor

I found this information on page _____.

Organize *resources that exist on the continental shelf and in the deep ocean by listing them below.*

Continental Shelf Deposits	Deep Ocean Water Deposits

CONNECT IT

Infer why retrieving resources from deep water is such a challenge.

_____

_____

_____

Oceanography
Section 2 Life in the Ocean

Skim *through Section 2 of your book. Read the headings and examine the illustrations. Write three questions that come to mind.*

1. _____

2. _____

3. _____

Review Vocabulary

Define nutrient *using its scientific meaning.*

nutrient _____

_____

New Vocabulary

Use your book to define each of the following terms. Then write a sentence to show its scientific meaning.

estuary _____

_____

_____

_____

reef _____

_____

_____

_____

Academic Vocabulary

Use a dictionary to define undergo. *Then write a sentence to show its scientific meaning.*

undergo _____

_____

_____

_____

Section 2 Life in the Ocean (continued)

<table>
<tr><td>**Main Idea**</td><td>**Details**</td></tr>
</table>

Life Processes

I found this information on page _____ .

Summarize *the ways that marine organisms obtain energy by completing the chart below.*

Name of process used to make food	How food is made	Example of producers	Example of consumers
Photosynthesis			
Chemosynthesis			

Ocean Life

I found this information on page _____ .

Classify *the organisms that live in the ocean. Complete the graphic organizer below to organize the types. Include descriptions and examples of each type.*

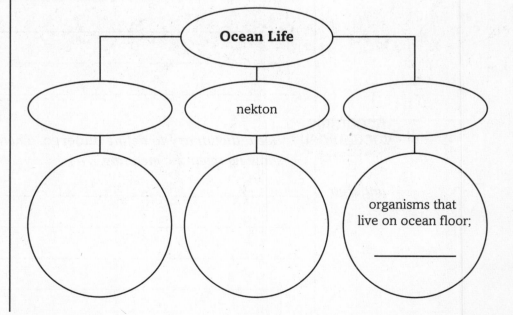

Section 2 Life in the Ocean (continued)

Main Idea _____ **Details** _____

Ocean Margin Habitats

I found this information on page _____.

Compare and contrast *ocean margin habitats. Identify four margin habitats and at least four examples of organisms that live in each one. Make a sketch of each habitat to help you remember.*

1. _____ 2. _____

Ocean Margin Habitats

3. _____ 4. _____

SYNTHESIZE IT Compare and contrast food webs that rely on chemosynthesis with food webs that depend on photosynthesis.

_____

_____

_____

_____

_____

Oceanography
Section 3 Ocean Pollution

Scan *Use the checklist below to preview Section 3 of your book.*

☐ Read all section titles.

☐ Read all bold words.

☐ Read all charts and graphs.

☐ Look at all of the pictures.

☐ Think about what you already know about ocean pollution.

Write three facts you discovered about ocean pollution.

1. _____

2. _____

3. _____

Review Vocabulary

Define runoff *using its scientific meaning.*

runoff

_____

_____

_____

New Vocabulary

Use your book to define pollution. *Then identify three types of pollution with which you are already familiar.*

pollution

_____

_____

_____

_____

Academic Vocabulary

Use a dictionary to define phenomenon *using its scientific meaning.*

phenomenon

_____

_____

Section 3 Ocean Pollution (continued)

Main Idea

Sources of Pollution

I found this information on page _____.

Details

Complete *the graphic organizer to identify five types of ocean pollution and their causes or sources.*

Types of Ocean Pollution	Causes of Ocean Pollution

Ocean Pollution

Section 3 Ocean Pollution (continued)

Main Idea

Details

Effects of Pollution

I found this information on page _____.

Summarize *the effects of pollution by completing the outline below.*

Effects of Pollution

  I. Delaware to North Carolina rivers and estuaries

    A. Type of pollution—_____

    B. Effects

      1. have killed billions of fish

      2. _____

        _____

  B. Florida

    A. Type of pollution—_____

    B. Effects

      1. _____

      2. _____

Controlling Pollution

I found this information on page _____.

List *five things you can do to reduce ocean pollution. Highlight the way you think would make the most impact.*

1. _____

2. _____

3. _____

4. _____

5. _____

CONNECT IT

Design a flow chart to show how pollution travels from your location to the ocean.

Tie It Together

Make a diagram of an ocean basin. Include

• the major features of the basin;

• the locations of continental shelf and deep-water resources;

• an example of a food chain;

• two examples of ocean pollution.

Oceanography   Chapter Wrap-Up

Now that you have read the chapter, think about what you have learned and complete the table below. Compare your previous answers with these.

1. Write an **A** if you agree with the statement.
2. Write a **D** if you disagree with the statement.

Oceanography	After You Read
• Sediment that originates on land rarely settles as far as the deep ocean floor.	
• Hot water streams out into surrounding seawater through holes and cracks along mid-ocean ridges.	
• The Sun is the source of nearly all of the energy used by organisms in the ocean.	
• Factories sometimes release chemicals into streams that eventually empty into the ocean.	

Review

Use this checklist to help you study.

☐ Review the information you included in your Foldable.

☐ Study your *Science Notebook* on this chapter.

☐ Study the definitions of vocabulary words.

☐ Review daily homework assignments.

☐ Re-read the chapter and review the charts, graphs, and illustrations.

☐ Review the Self Check at the end of each section.

☐ Look over the Chapter Review at the end of the chapter.

SUMMARIZE IT
After reading this chapter, identify three things that you have learned about oceanography.

_____

_____

_____

_____

Name _____ **Date** _____

Our Impact on Land

Before You Read

Before you read the chapter, respond to these statements.

   1. Write an **A** if you agree with the statement.

   2. Write a **D** if you disagree with the statement.

Before You Read	Our Impact on Land
	• *Population explosion* is a term that describes how the world population has grown rapidly in recent history.
	• By the time you are 75 years old, you will have produced enough garbage to equal the mass of 11 African elephants.
	• To feed the growing population, farmers are using higher yielding seeds.
	• Most deforestation occurs in developed countries.

FOLDABLES TM
Study Organizer

Construct the Foldable as directed at the beginning of this chapter.

Science Journal

Write three ways that you can reduce the amount of trash you throw in the garbage.

_____

_____

_____

_____

_____

Our Impact on Land

Section 1 Population Impact on the Environment

Scan *Section 1 of your book. Write three facts that you discovered about world population as you scanned the section.*

1. _____

2. _____

3. _____

Review Vocabulary

Define natural resource *using your book or a dictionary.*

natural resource _____

_____

New Vocabulary

Use your book or a dictionary to define each key term. Then use each in a scientific sentence.

population _____

_____

_____

carrying capacity _____

_____

_____

pollutant _____

_____

_____

Academic Vocabulary

Use a dictionary to define environment.

environment _____

_____

Section 1 Population Impact on the Environment (continued)

Main Idea

Population and Carrying Capacity

I found this information on page _____.

Details

Model *population growth of modern humans on the grid below. Use the facts given in the five sentences.*

1. Human population was _____ in 1700 A.D.

2. Human population first reached 1 billion in _____

3. In 1960 A.D., human population was _____

4. Human population reached 6.1 billion in _____

5. The population is expected to reach _____ by 2050 A.D.

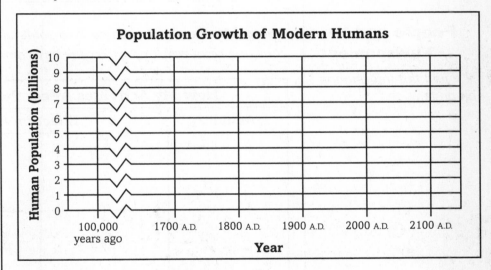

I found this information on page _____.

Define carrying capacity. *Hypothesize about some factors that limit the carrying capacity and things humans could do to increase Earth's carrying capacity.*

Carrying Capacity		
Limits	Definition	Ways to increase it

Section 1 Population Impact on the Environment (continued)

Main Idea

I found this information on page _____.

Details

Create *a concept map to summarize reasons why there is such concern about the growing population.*

┌───┐
│   │
│   │
│   │
│   │
│   │
│   │
└───┘

People and the Environment

I found this information on page _____.

Complete *the chart to show how some of your daily activities consume resources and affect the environment.*

How My Activities Affect the Environment	
Activity	Effect on Environment

CONNECT IT

Describe how you might be affected at school if suddenly there were twice as many students.

_____

_____

_____

_____

Our Impact on Land
Section 2 Using Land

Skim *Section 2 of your book. Read the headings and look at the pictures. Write three questions that come to mind.*

1. _____

2. _____

3. _____

Review Vocabulary
Define erosion *using your book or a dictionary.*

erosion

_____

_____

New Vocabulary
Skim through the section to find each term, and then give a definition for each from your text.

stream discharge

_____

_____

sanitary landfill

_____

_____

hazardous waste

_____

_____

enzyme

_____

_____

Academic Vocabulary
Use a dictionary to define impact.

impact

_____

_____

Section 2 Using Land (continued)

Main Idea

Land Usage

I found this information on page _____.

Details

Organize *information about land usage in the outline.*

Land uses and their environmental problems

   A. Agriculture

      1. _____

      2. Increases soil erosion.

   B. Forest Resource Use

      1. _____

      2. _____

   C. Development

      1. Paving stops water from soaking into soil and causes flooding.

      2. _____

   D. Landfills

      1. _____

      2. _____

I found this information on page _____.

Create *a diagram of a sanitary landfill. Be sure to label each element in your plan.*

Describe *how your landfill will keep pollution from entering the environment.*

_____

_____

_____

Name _____ **Date** _____

Section 2 Using Land (continued)

◁Main Idea▷   ◁Details▷

**Hazardous
Wastes**

*I found this information
on page* _____.

Summarize *characteristics and effects of hazardous waste.*

Characteristics:	Hazardous waste	Effects:

*I found this information
on page* _____.

Identify *four actions by the government and citizens since 1980
that relate to hazardous wastes.*

1. _____

_____

2. _____

_____

3. _____

_____

4. _____

_____

**Natural
Preserves**

*I found this information
on page* _____.

Classify *the three types of national preserves.*

1. _____

2. _____

3. _____

CONNECT IT List three kinds of hazardous wastes found in many homes. Identify
the characteristic that makes each hazardous.

_____

_____

Our Impact on Land
Section 3 Conserving Resources

Skim *the headings and boldfaced terms in Section 3. Then make three predictions about what you will learn.*

1. _____

2. _____

3. _____

Review Vocabulary

Define consumption. *Then use it in a sentence to show its scientific meaning.*

consumption

_____

_____

_____

New Vocabulary

Define the following terms. Then use each in a scientific sentence.

conservation

_____

_____

_____

composting

_____

_____

_____

recycling

_____

_____

Academic Vocabulary

Use a dictionary to define recover.

recover

_____

_____

Section 3 Conserving Resources (continued)

| Main Idea | Details |

Resource Use

I found this information on page _____.

Complete *the graphic organizer below to show the benefits of conserving resources.*

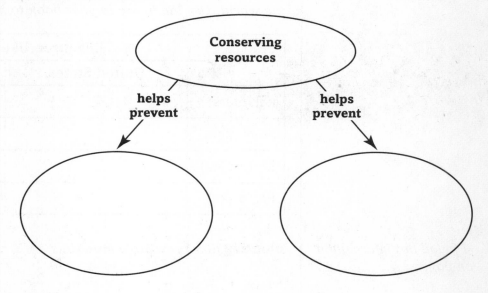

Reduce, Reuse, Recycle

I found this information on page _____.

Classify *various conservation activities by providing an example of each under the correct heading.*

Reduce	Reuse	Recycle

Complete *the statements with the correct percent from the bank.*

    20%   40%   58%   74%

Paper makes up _____ of the mass of trash. Recycling this

paper would use _____ less water and make _____ less

pollution than making new paper.

If everyone in the United States composted, it would reduce the

trash in landfills by _____.

Section 3 Conserving Resources (continued)

Main Idea

Details

I found this information on page _____.

Compare *the use of resources by the average person in the United States with the resources used by the average person elsewhere in the world. Use the figure in your book to help you.*

Resource Use		
	United States	Rest of world
Oil (liters)		
Steel (kg)		
Metals (kg)		
Paper (kg)		

I found this information on page _____.

Identify *four recyclable materials.*

1. _____ 2. _____

3. _____ 4. _____

Summarize *challenges to developing good recycling programs.*

1. _____

_____

2. _____

_____

3. _____

_____

CONNECT IT

Think about the resources listed in the chart above. Describe a strategy for reducing the amount of oil, steel, metals, or paper that you use.

_____

_____

_____

_____

Tie It Together

Create *an ad campaign that promotes the conservation of resources. Your campaign may be*

- a video,
- a pamphlet,
- posters, or
- flyers.

Choose an audience for your campaign: young children, senior citizens, your peers, your school, or your community.

Then create an informative and inspiring message. Write your message below.

_____

_____

_____

_____

_____

_____

_____

_____

_____

_____

_____

_____

_____

_____

_____

_____

Our Impact on Land Chapter Wrap-Up

Now that you have read the chapter, think about what you have learned and complete the table below. Compare your previous answers with these.

1. Write an **A** if you agree with the statement.
2. Write a **D** if you disagree with the statement.

Our Impact on Land	After You Read
• *Population explosion* is a term that describes how the world population has grown rapidly in recent history.	
• By the time you are 75 years old, you will have produced enough garbage to equal the mass of 11 African elephants.	
• To feed the growing population, farmers are using higher yielding seeds.	
• Most deforestation occurs in developed countries.	

Review

Use this checklist to help you study.

☐ Review the information you included in your Foldable.

☐ Study your *Science Notebook* on this chapter.

☐ Study the definitions of vocabulary words.

☐ Review daily homework assignments.

☐ Re-read the chapter and review the charts, graphs, and illustrations.

☐ Review the Self Check at the end of each section.

☐ Look over the Chapter Review at the end of the chapter.

SUMMARIZE IT
After reading this chapter, identify three things that you have learned about our impact on land.

_____

_____

_____

_____

Our Impact on Water and Air

Before You Read

Preview the chapter, including section titles and section headings. Complete the chart by listing at least one idea for each section in each column.

K What I know	W What I want to find out

FOLDABLES™
Study Organizer

Construct the Foldable as directed at the beginning of this chapter.

Science Journal

Hypothesize what happens to the water in your home after the water goes down the drain.

_____

_____

_____

_____

_____

_____

_____

Our Impact on Water and Air
Section 1 Water Pollution

Objectives *Review the objectives for Section 1. Write three questions that come to mind from reading these statements. Look for answers to these questions as you read the section.*

1. _____

2. _____

3. _____

 **Review Vocabulary**

Define pollution *using your book or a dictionary.*

pollution

_____

_____

 **New Vocabulary**

Read the definitions below. Write the correct key term on the blank in the left column.

_____ a chemical that helps plants grow

_____ water that goes into drains and contains human waste, household detergents, and soaps

_____ a substance that destroys pests

_____ pollution that enters water from a specific location such as drainpipes or ditches

_____ pollution that enters a body of water from a large area, which might include lawns, construction sites, and roads

 **Academic Vocabulary**

Use a dictionary to define chemical.

chemical

_____

_____

Section 1 Water Pollution (continued)

Main Idea · Details

Importance of Clean Water

I found this information on page _____ .

Complete *the paragraph about clean water.*

Clean water is important because all _____ need

it to live. Plants need water to _____ . People must

_____ water every day. Many organisms, such as

fish, _____ in water. _____ can

damage organisms. Animals might die or be more likely to get a

_____ .

Sources of Water Pollution

I found this information on page _____ .

Summarize *the effects of each source of water pollution by completing the chart.*

Sources of Water Pollution and Their Effects	
Source	Effects
Sediment	
Pesticides	
Fertilizers	
Human waste/ sewage	
Metals	
Oil and gasoline	
Heat	

Section 1 Water Pollution (continued)

Main Idea

Details

Reducing Water Pollution

I found this information on page _____.

Compare and contrast *the Clean Water Act of 1987 and the Safe Drinking Water Act of 1996. Complete the Venn diagram with two facts about each act.*

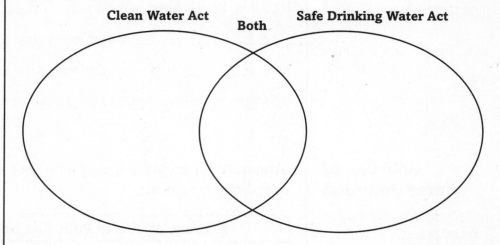

How can you help?

I found this information on page _____.

Create *two original drawings that illustrate (1) how people can help to reduce water pollution and (2) how people can help to conserve water. Include captions for each drawing.*

Reduce Water Pollution	Conserve Water
Caption:	Caption:

CONNECT IT Identify three ways you use water in your daily life that are not discussed in the book. Choose one of your suggestions, and explain how you can change the way you use water to help conserve this vital resource.

_____

_____

_____

Name _____ Date _____

Our Impact on Water and Air
Section 2 Air Pollution

Scan *Use the checklist below to preview Section 2 of your book.*

☐ Read all section headings.

☐ Read all bold words.

☐ Look at all of the pictures and read their labels.

☐ Think about what you already know about air pollution.

Write two facts that you discovered about air pollution.

1. _____

2. _____

Review Vocabulary

Define ozone layer *using your book or a dictionary.*

ozone layer

_____

_____

New Vocabulary

Write the correct key term on the blank in the left column.

_____   acidic moisture that falls to Earth as rain or snow

_____   colorless, odorless gas in car exhaust that contributes to air pollution

_____   substance with a pH higher than 7

_____   device that removes sulfur dioxide from smoke produced by a coal-burning power plant

_____   substance with a pH below 7

_____   used to describe how acidic or basic a substance is

_____   fine particles such as dust, pollen, mold, ash, and soot that are in the air

_____   hazy, yellowish-brown smog that sometimes occurs over cities

Academic Vocabulary

Use a dictionary to define convert *using its scientific meaning.*

convert

_____

_____

Section 2 Air Pollution (continued)

◁Main Idea▷

◁Details▷

Causes of Air Pollution

I found this information on page _____.

Classify *the causes of air pollution discussed in the book as* Natural *or* Produced by Humans. *List each cause in the chart.*

Natural	Produced by Humans

What is smog?

I found this information on page _____.

Sequence *steps in the formation of* smog.

1.	
2.	
3.	
4.	

Acid Rain

I found this information on page _____.

Create *an original drawing in the box to show how* acid rain *forms. Add labels to your drawing to identify what it shows.*

Section 2 Air Pollution (continued)

◀Main Idea▶   ◀Details▶

CFCs

I found this information on page _____ .

Summarize *why CFCs are harmful.*

_____
_____
_____
_____
_____

Air Pollution and Your Health

I found this information on page _____ .

Summarize *the health effects of air pollutants in the chart.*

Pollutant	Health Effects
Carbon monoxide	
Acid rain	
Particulates	

Reducing Air Pollution

I found this information on page _____ .

Complete *the graphic organizer about reducing air pollution.*

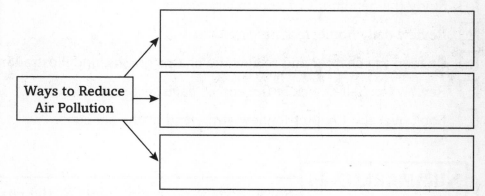

Ways to Reduce Air Pollution

SYNTHESIZE IT Why would setting the thermostat in your home at a lower temperature in winter and a higher temperature in summer help reduce air pollution?

_____
_____

Our Impact on Water and Air
Chapter Wrap-Up

Review the ideas you listed in the chart at the beginning of the chapter. Cross out any incorrect information in the first column. Then complete the chart by filling in the third column. How do your ideas now compare with those you wrote at the beginning of the chapter?

K What I know	W What I want to find out	L What I learned

Review

Use this checklist to help you study.

☐ Review the information you included in your Foldable.

☐ Study your *Science Notebook* on this chapter.

☐ Study the definitions of vocabulary words.

☐ Review daily homework assignments.

☐ Re-read the chapter and review the charts, graphs, and illustrations.

☐ Review the Self Check at the end of each section.

☐ Look over the Chapter Review at the end of the chapter.

SUMMARIZE IT
Summarize three main points of the chapter.

_____

_____

_____

_____

Name _____ **Date** _____

Exploring Space

Before You Read

Preview the chapter, including section titles and the section headings. Complete the chart by listing at least one idea for each of the three sections in each column.

K What I know	W What I want to find out

FOLDABLES™
Study Organizer

Construct the Foldable as directed at the beginning of this chapter.

Science Journal

Do you think space exploration is worth the risk and expense? Explain why.

_____

_____

_____

_____

_____

_____

_____

Exploring Space

Section 1 Radiation from Space

Evaluate *the objectives found in* What You'll Learn *for Section 1. Write three questions that come to mind from reading these statements.*

1. _____

2. _____

3. _____

Review Vocabulary

Define telescope *using your book or a dictionary.*

telescope _____

_____

New Vocabulary

Use your book or a dictionary to define the vocabulary terms.

electromagnetic spectrum _____

_____

refracting telescope _____

_____

reflecting telescope _____

_____

observatory _____

_____

radio telescope _____

_____

Academic Vocabulary

Use a dictionary to define visible.

visible _____

Section 1 Radiation from Space (continued)

⟨ Main Idea ⟩	⟨ Details ⟩
Electromagnetic Waves *I found this information on page _____ .*	**List** *seven forms of* electromagnetic radiation.

1. _____   5. _____

2. _____   6. _____

3. _____   7. _____

4. _____

Compare and contrast short wavelength radiation *with* long wavelength radiation *by completing the chart below.*

	Short Wavelength	**Long Wavelength**
Sketch of each wave		
Description of frequency		

Optical Telescopes

I found this information on page _____ .

Compare *a refracting telescope* with *a reflecting telescope.*

- Use your book to help you draw cross-sections of each telescope.
- Use arrows to indicate the path taken by light in each type.
- Label the eyepiece lens, focal point, and any other mirrors or lenses.
- Model the shapes of a convex lens and a concave mirror.

refracting telescope	**reflecting telescope**
convex lens	**concave mirror**

Section 1 Radiation from Space (continued)

Main Idea	Details

Optical Telescopes

I found this information on page _____.

Summarize *information about the* Hubble Space Telescope *by completing the paragraph.*

In _____, the _____

was launched. Scientists expected clear pictures from this

_____ telescope because it was _____

_____. However, a mistake was made when

the telescope's _____, so it did

not make _____. Repair missions were made in

(years) _____, when small _____

were added to correct the images.

Radio Telescopes

I found this information on page _____.

Organize *information about* radio telescopes *in the chart below.*

Radio telescopes
Purpose:
Design:
Collect information used to: 1.   3.   2.

CONNECT IT Radio waves from space have been studied for decades, but scientists have yet to find signs of intelligent life. Suggest several explanations for this.

_____

_____

_____

Exploring Space
Section 2 Early Space Missions

Predict *three things that you think might be discussed in this section after reading its headings.*

1. _____

_____

2. _____

_____

3. _____

_____

Review Vocabulary *Write the correct vocabulary term next to each definition.*

_____ force that propels an aircraft or missile

New Vocabulary

_____ curved path followed by a satellite as it revolves around an object

_____ space mission with goal of landing a human on the Moon's surface

_____ special engine that can work in space and burns liquid or solid fuel

_____ space mission with goals of connecting spacecraft in orbit and investigating the effects of space travel on the human body

_____ any object that revolves around another object in space

_____ space mission with goal of orbiting a piloted spacecraft around Earth and bringing it back safely

_____ instrument that gathers information and sends it back to Earth

Academic Vocabulary **Define** *the scientific meaning of* goal *using a dictionary.*

goal _____

_____

Section 2 Early Space Missions (continued)

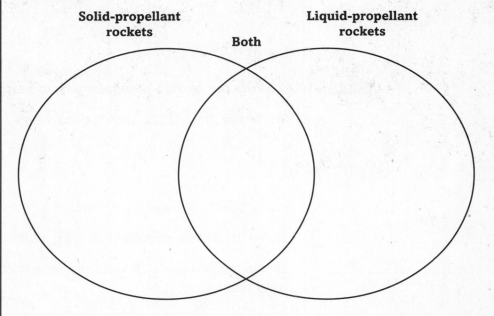

Main Idea

The First Missions into Space

I found this information on page _____.

Details

Compare and contrast *the two types of rockets by completing the Venn diagram with the information below.*

- can be shut down and restarted
- do not require air for operation
- liquid fuel and oxidizer stored in separate tanks
- preferred for long-term space missions

- gases thrust it forward
- rubberlike fuel contains oxidizer
- generally simpler
- cannot be shut down once ignited

Solid-propellant rockets   **Both**   **Liquid-propellant rockets**

I found this information on page _____.

Model *the path of a satellite. Draw a satellite in orbit around Earth. Show the complete path of the satellite and the path it would take if it were not affected by gravity.*

Section 2 Early Space Missions (continued)

Main Idea | Details

Space Probes

I found this information on page _____ .

Compare *the advantages and disadvantages of space probes with spacecraft piloted by humans.*

Comparison of Space Probes to Piloted Spacecraft	
Advantages	Disadvantages

Moon Quest

I found this information on page _____ .

Create *a time line of the United States' quest to reach the Moon by identifying an event that corresponds to each date.*

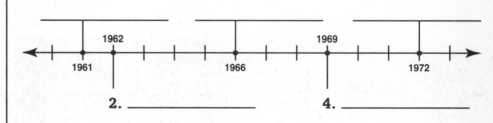

1. _____ 3. _____ 5. _____

1961   1962   1966   1969   1972

2. _____   4. _____

CONNECT IT

Design a plan for a space mission to take humans to Mars. Analyze challenges the crew would have to face. Develop a simple program to help prepare the crew to face these challenges.

_____

_____

_____

_____

_____

Exploring Space
Section 3 Current and Future Space Missions

Skim *through Section 3 of your text. Read the headings and examine the illustrations. Write three questions that come to mind. Try to answer your questions as you read.*

1. _____
   _____

2. _____
   _____

3. _____
   _____

Review Vocabulary

Use cosmonaut *in a sentence that shows its scientific meaning.*

cosmonaut _____
   _____

New Vocabulary

Use the following key terms in original sentences to show their scientific meaning.

space shuttle _____

space station _____
   _____

Academic Vocabulary

Define *the scientific meaning of* technology *using a dictionary.*

technology _____
   _____

Section 3 Current and Future Space Missions (continued)

<table>
<tr><td>**Main Idea**</td><td colspan="2">**Details**</td></tr>
<tr>
<td>

The Space Shuttle

I found this information on page _____.

</td>
<td colspan="2">

Summarize *characteristics of the* space shuttle *below.*

</td>
</tr>
</table>

Engines:	Cargo bay:
Landings:	**Reusability:**

Exploring Mars

I found this information on page _____.

Organize *information about missions to Mars by completing the diagram. Identify each probe by its name and mission.*

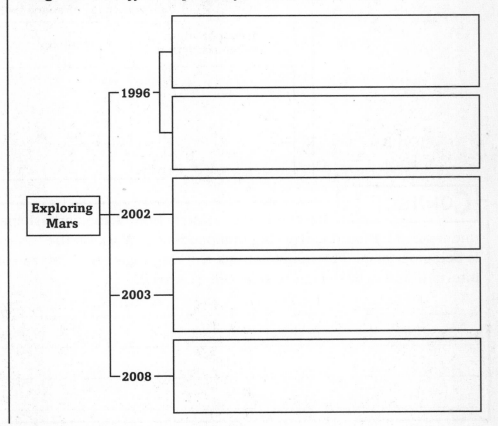

Section 3 Current and Future Space Missions (continued)

Main Idea	Details

Exploring the Moon and *Cassini*

I found this information on page _____.

Complete *the chart with information about the* Lunar Prospector *and* Cassini *spacecraft.*

Spacecraft	Launch Date	Destination	Goals
Lunar Prospector			
Cassini			

I found this information on page _____.

Organize *information by identifying an example of technology developed for space programs that is useful in everyday life.*

Everyday uses of space technology

transportation and construction	medicine	law enforcement and safety

CONNECT IT

Research and construction of the earliest space stations was undertaken by nations working independently. Work on the International Space Station is being performed by many nations working together. Analyze some benefits to such international cooperation in scientific research.

_____

_____

_____

_____

Tie It Together

Synthesize It

Much of today's planetary research is carried out using remote-controlled rovers that are monitored and maneuvered by scientists on Earth. Suppose that you could design a remote-controlled rover to conduct research on a planet or the Moon.

• Draw a sketch of your rover below.
• Identify features you would include on your rover.
• Explain why you would include each feature.
• Use what you have learned about space technologies in this section.

Exploring Space   Chapter Wrap-Up

Review the ideas you listed in the chart at the beginning of the chapter. Cross out any incorrect information in the first column. Then complete the chart by filling in the third column.

K What I know	W What I want to find out	L What I learned

Review

Use this checklist to help you study.

- ☐ Review the information you included in your Foldable.
- ☐ Study your *Science Notebook* on this chapter.
- ☐ Study the definitions of vocabulary words.
- ☐ Review daily homework assignments.
- ☐ Re-read the chapter and review the charts, graphs, and illustrations.
- ☐ Review the Self Check at the end of each section.
- ☐ Look over the Chapter Review at the end of the chapter.

SUMMARIZE IT
After reading this chapter, identify three things that you have learned about exploring space.

_____

_____

_____

_____

Name _____ **Date** _____

The Sun-Earth-Moon System

Before You Read

Before you read the chapter, respond to these statements.

    1. Write an **A** if you agree with the statement.

    2. Write a **D** if you disagree with the statement.

Before You Read	The Sun-Earth-Moon System
	• The Sun appears to move across the sky each day.
	• The spinning of Earth on its axis is rotation.
	• The Moon's rotation and revolution take the same amount of time, so the same side of the Moon always faces Earth.
	• No evidence of water has been found on the Moon.

 *Construct the Foldable as directed at the beginning of this chapter.*

Science Journal

Rotation or revolution—which motion of Earth brings morning and which brings summer?

_____

_____

_____

_____

_____

_____

The Sun-Earth-Moon System

Section 1 Earth

Scan *the tables and illustrations in Section 1, and write three questions you have about Earth.*

1. _____

_____

2. _____

_____

3. _____

_____

Use orbit *in a sentence that reflects its scientific meaning.*

orbit

_____

_____

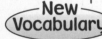

Write the correct vocabulary term on each blank.

_____ spinning of Earth on its axis, which causes day and night to occur

_____ Earth's yearly orbit around the Sun

_____ imaginary line around which Earth spins

_____ elongated, closed curve, such as Earth's orbit around the Sun

_____ occurs when the Sun is directly above Earth's equator and the number of daylight and nighttime hours are nearly equal

_____ day when the Sun reaches its greatest distance north or south of the equator

_____ round, three-dimensional object

Define maintain *using a dictionary.*

maintain

_____

_____

Section 1 Earth (continued)

| **Main Idea** | **Details** |

Properties of Earth

I found this information on page _____.

Label *the diagram of Earth.*

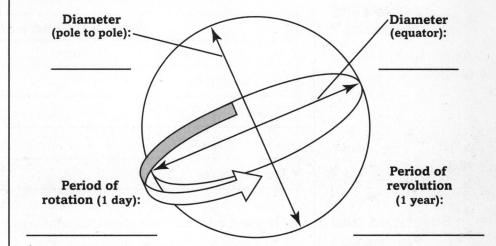

Diameter (pole to pole):
_____

Diameter (equator):
_____

Period of rotation (1 day):
_____

Period of revolution (1 year):
_____

Magnetic Field

I found this information on page _____.

Compare *Earth's magnetic poles with its rotational poles by drawing them on the circle below. Label Earth's:*

- rotational axis
- rotational poles
- north magnetic pole
- south magnetic pole

- the difference in degrees between the magnetic and rotational poles

Summarize *why Earth has a magnetic field.*

_____

_____

Section 1 **Earth** (continued)

Main Idea

What causes changing seasons?

I found this information on page _____ .

Details

Compare *facts about summer and winter in the chart.*

Seasonal Conditions		
	Summer	**Winter**
Hemisphere tilts		
Hours of daylight		
Solar radiation		
Temperatures		

Solstices and Equinoxes

I found this information on page _____ .

Compare *and contrast* solstices *and* equinoxes *by completing the Venn diagram using the phrases below.*

- caused by tilt of Earth's axis
- daylight hours and nighttime hours nearly equal
- longest or shortest period of daylight of the year
- occur twice yearly
- Sun at 90° angle to equator
- Sun reaches greatest distance from equator

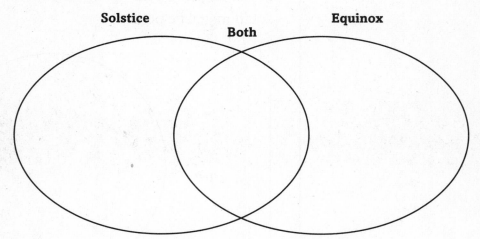

Solstice   **Both**   **Equinox**

CONNECT IT It takes Earth one year to make a complete revolution around the Sun. Determine how much time passes between one spring equinox and the next. Explain your reasoning.

_____

_____

The Sun-Earth-Moon System
Section 2 The Moon—Earth's Satellite

Predict *three things that might be discussed in Section 2 based on its title and headings.*

1. _____

2. _____

3. _____

Review Vocabulary

Define mantle *to show its scientific meaning.*

mantle _____

_____

New Vocabulary

Write the correct vocabulary term next to each definition.

_____ different ways the Moon appears from Earth

_____ occurs when the lit side of the moon is not visible; the moon is between Earth and the Sun

_____ describes the Moon when more of its lighted portion is visible each night

_____ occurs when all of the Moon's surface that faces Earth is lit

_____ describes the Moon when less of its lighted portion is visible each night

_____ occurs when the Moon moves between the Sun and Earth and casts a shadow over part of Earth

_____ occurs when Earth moves between the Sun and the Moon and casts a shadow on the Moon

_____ dark, flat regions on the Moon that formed as lava spread over the surface

Academic Vocabulary

Use the term cycle *in a sentence that reflects its scientific meaning.*

cycle _____

_____

Section 2 The Moon—Earth's Satellite (continued)

Main Idea	Details
Motions of the Moon *I found this information on page _____.*	**Describe** *why the face of the Moon that we see does not change.* _____ _____ _____
Phases of the Moon *I found this information on page _____.*	**Analyze** *the diagram below. Imagine that you are standing on Earth and that the Sun's rays are coming from the direction shown. Draw a picture showing how the moon would look from Earth at each of the labeled positions. The first one has been done for you.*

Sunlight

1	2	3	4
The Moon cannot be seen from Earth. Its opposite side is lit.			
5	6	7	8

⟨ Main Idea ⟩ ————————— ⟨ Details ⟩ ————————

Eclipses

I found this information on page _____.

Compare *the alignments that cause solar and lunar eclipses by drawing diagrams of the positions of the Sun, the Moon, and Earth relative to one another. Show how the shadow is cast in each case.*

Solar Eclipse

Lunar Eclipse

Inside the Moon

I found this information on page _____.

Summarize *the Moon's structure according to one model.*

Surface and Interior of the Moon	
Zone	**Description**
Crust	
Upper Mantle	
Lower Mantle	
Core	

SUMMARIZE IT

Summarize the impact theory of how the Moon formed.

_____

_____

_____

_____

The Sun-Earth-Moon System
Section 3 Exploring Earth's Moon

Objectives *Review the objectives for Section 3. Write two questions that come to mind.*

1. _____

2. _____

Review Vocabulary

Define comet *using your book or a dictionary. Then write a sentence or make a sketch to show its scientific meaning.*

comet

_____

_____

_____

_____

New Vocabulary

Define impact basin *using your book or a dictionary. Then sketch how an impact basin forms.*

impact basin

_____

_____

_____

_____

Academic Vocabulary

Use a dictionary to define core *as it relates to planets and moons. Then sketch the Moon, and show where you think its core is.*

core

_____

_____

_____

_____

Section 3 Exploring Earth's Moon (continued)

| Main Idea | Details |

Missions to the Moon

I found this information on page _____.

Distinguish *between the following Moon missions by indicating when they took place and what they accomplished.*

Mission	Year	Accomplishment
Luna 3		
Surveyor 1		
Lunar Orbiters		
Apollo 8		
Apollo 11		
Apollo 15		
Apollo 17		

I found this information on page _____.

Organize *information about* Clementine's *mission by outlining it below.*

Clementine's mission

   I. Objectives

      A. _____

      B. _____

  II. Instruments

      A. _____

      B. _____

 III. Discoveries

      A. _____

      B. _____

Section 3 Exploring Earth's Moon (continued)

Main Idea	Details

I found this information on page _____.

Organize *information about the Lunar Prospector by completing the diagram.*

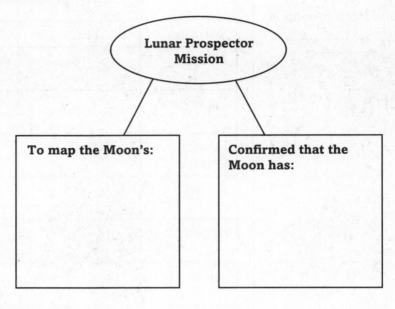

Lunar Prospector Mission

To map the Moon's:

Confirmed that the Moon has:

Analyze *why the presence of water on the Moon would be a benefit to humans.*

_____

_____

_____

SYNTHESIZE IT Missions to the Moon have included some with astronauts and some without astronauts. Predict whether astronauts will be sent on Moon missions in the future. Support your position with three facts or examples.

_____

_____

_____

_____

Tie It Together

Synthesize It

Suppose that you are on a mission to explore the Moon. In the spaces provided, describe what you think you will observe from each location.

From the windows of your spacecraft orbiting the Moon

_____

_____

_____

_____

_____

On the Moon's surface near the Moon's equator

_____

_____

_____

_____

_____

On the surface near the Moon's south pole

_____

_____

_____

_____

_____

The Earth-Moon-Sun System
Chapter Wrap-Up

Now that you have read the chapter, think about what you have learned and complete the table below. Compare your previous answers with these.

1. Write an **A** if you agree with the statement.
2. Write a **D** if you disagree with the statement.

The Sun-Earth-Moon System	After You Read
• The Sun appears to move across the sky each day.	
• The spinning of Earth on its axis is rotation.	
• The Moon's rotation and revolution take the same amount of time, so the same side of the Moon always faces Earth.	
• No evidence of water has been found on the Moon.	

Review
Use this checklist to help you study.

- ☐ Review the information you included in your Foldable.
- ☐ Study your *Science Notebook* on this chapter.
- ☐ Study the definitions of vocabulary words.
- ☐ Review daily homework assignments.
- ☐ Re-read the chapter and review the charts, graphs, and illustrations.
- ☐ Review the Self Check at the end of each section.
- ☐ Look over the Chapter Review at the end of the chapter.

SUMMARIZE IT After reading this chapter, identify three things that you have learned about the Sun-Earth-Moon system.

_____

_____

_____

_____

Copyright © Glencoe/McGraw-Hill, a division of The McGraw-Hill Companies, Inc.

The Solar System

Before You Read

Before you read the chapter, respond to these statements.

1. Write an **A** if you agree with the statement.
2. Write a **D** if you disagree with the statement.

Before You Read	The Solar System
	• The planets revolve around Earth.
	• The solar system is more than 4.6 billion years old.
	• Mercury has an atmosphere similar to Earth's.
	• Uranus has craters and deep valleys.
	• Earth is the only planet known to be able to support life.

Construct the Foldable as directed at the beginning of this chapter.

Science Journal

If you could command the Keck telescope, what would you view? Describe what you would see.

_____

_____

_____

_____

_____

_____

_____

The Solar System
Section 1 The Solar System

Skim *the headings in Section 1. Write three things you expect to learn in Section 1.*

1. _____

   _____

2. _____

   _____

3. _____

   _____

Define system *using your book or a dictionary. Give an example of a system.*

system _____

_____

Write a scientific sentence describing the solar system.

solar system _____

_____

Define contract *as a verb, using a dictionary. Then rewrite the following sentence, using the word* contracted.

Over time, the cloud of gas and dust became smaller, forming a large, tightly packed, spinning disk.

contract _____

_____

_____

_____

Name _____ Date _____

Section 1 The Solar System (continued)

Main Idea

Ideas About the Solar System

I found this information on page _____.

I found this information on page _____.

I found this information on page _____.

Details

Contrast *the Earth-centered model of the solar system and the Sun-centered model of the solar system in the chart below.*

	Earth-centered	**Sun-centered**
How many planets are in the system?		
Describe motions in the system.		

Evaluate *how Galileo's discoveries provided evidence for the Sun-centered model of the solar system. Complete the statements.*

Galileo discovered that the planet _____ went through

_____ like our _____. These changes could

occur only _____.

Create *a drawing of the solar system.*

• Draw and label the Sun and the planets in the correct order.
• Identify which planets were included in the Earth-centered model of the solar system by putting a check mark beside those.

Section 1 The Solar System (continued)

Main Idea	Details

How the Solar System Formed

I found this information on page _____.

Sequence *the steps in the formation of the solar system.*

1. _____

   _____

2. _____

   _____

3. _____

   _____

4. _____

   _____

I found this information on page _____.

Classify *the eight planets as inner or outer planets, using the chart below. Identify a characteristic of each group of planets.*

The Eight Planets		
	Inner	Outer
Names of Planets		
Characteristics		

SUMMARIZE IT Summarize how ideas about the structure and motions of the solar system changed over time.

_____

_____

_____

_____

The Solar System
Section 2 The Inner Planets

Scan *the headings of Section 2. Write a question for each heading.*

Mercury: _____

Venus: _____

Earth: _____

Mars: _____

Review Vocabulary **Define** space probe *using your book or a dictionary.*

space probe

_____

_____

New Vocabulary *Write a scientific sentence using each vocabulary term.*

Mercury

_____

_____

Venus

_____

_____

Earth

_____

_____

Mars

_____

_____

Academic Vocabulary *Use a dictionary to define* reveal.

reveal

_____

_____

Section 2 The Inner Planets (continued)

Main Idea	Details

Mercury

I found this information on page _____.

Organize *key facts about Mercury. Complete the chart.*

Mercury	
Location	
Surface	
Core	
Atmosphere	
Temperature	
Explored By	

Venus

I found this information on page _____.

Complete *the graphic organizer to identify key features of Venus.*

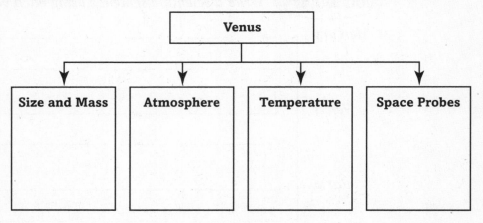

Earth

I found this information on page _____.

Summarize *unique features of Earth that allow it to support life.*

_____

_____

_____

_____

_____

Section 2 The Inner Planets (continued)

Main Idea   **Details**

Mars   **Summarize** *important information about Mars.*

*I found this information
on page _____.*

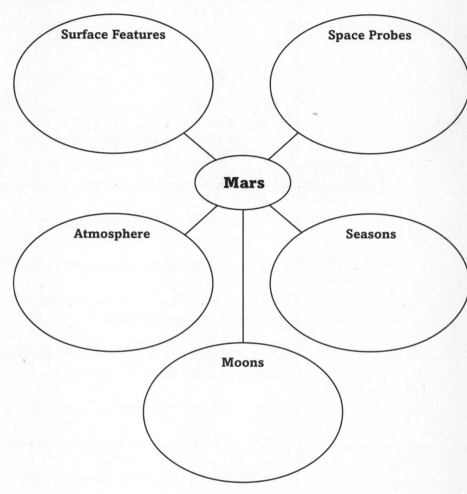

SYNTHESIZE IT

Compare and contrast the inner planets. Choose one feature, such as temperature, size, or atmosphere, and write a paragraph comparing and contrasting this feature for the four inner planets.

_____

_____

_____

_____

The Solar System
Section 3 The Outer Planets

Skim *Section 3. Predict two ways in which the outer planets differ from the inner planets.*

1. _____

_____

2. _____

_____

Review Vocabulary

Define *the word* moon *using a dictionary or your book.*

moon

_____

New Vocabulary

Label each definition with the correct vocabulary term.

_____ the seventh planet from the Sun; large and gaseous, with a distinct bluish-green color

_____ largest planet and fifth from the Sun; contains more mass than all of the other planets combined

_____ dwarf planet; has a solid icy-rock surface

_____ giant, high-pressure storm in Jupiter's atmosphere

_____ usually the eighth planet from the Sun; large and gaseous, with rings that vary in thickness

_____ second-largest planet and sixth from the Sun; has a complex ring system and at least 31 moons

Academic Vocabulary

Define survey *as a verb, using a dictionary. Then use this term in a sentence related to the topic of Section 3.*

survey

_____

_____

Section 3 The Outer Planets (continued)

Main Idea

Details

Jupiter

I found this information on page _____.

Identify *the space probes that have explored Jupiter.*

_____

_____

_____

Complete *the chart to identify key facts about Jupiter.*

Jupiter	
Atmosphere	
Moons	

Saturn

I found this information on page _____.

Organize *key facts about Saturn.*

Saturn	
Space Probes	
Atmosphere	
Rings	
Moons	

Section 3 The Outer Planets (continued)

Main Idea	Details

Uranus

I found this information on page _____.

Summarize *details about Uranus in the graphic organizer.*

Types of Mixtures

Neptune

I found this information on page _____.

Complete *the chart of key facts about Neptune.*

Neptune	
Atmosphere	
Moons	

Dwarf Planets

I found this information on page _____.

Summarize *the features of the dwarf planets.*

_____

_____

_____

_____

CONNECT IT Summarize the major features that distinguish the outer planets from the inner planets.

_____

_____

_____

The Solar System

Section 4 Other Objects in the Solar System

Scan *the title and headings in Section 4. Write a sentence that describes what you think will be covered in the section.*

_____

_____

_____

Review Vocabulary

crater

Write a scientific sentence using the term crater.

_____

_____

New Vocabulary

comet

Define *each term using your book or a dictionary.*

_____

_____

meteor

_____

_____

meteorite

_____

_____

asteroid

_____

_____

Academic Vocabulary

approach

Define approach, *using a dictionary. Then locate a sentence in Section 4 that uses the word or a form of the word.*

_____

_____

_____

Section 4 Other Objects in the Solar System (continued)

Main Idea	Details

Comets

I found this information on page _____.

Summarize *two facts about the Oort Cloud.*

1. _____

2. _____

Model *a comet. Label its* nucleus, coma, *and* tail. *Show the* solar wind *coming from the Sun and where the Sun is in relation to the comet's tail.*

Meteoroids, Meteors, and Meteorites

I found this information on page _____.

Distinguish *between* meteoroids, meteors, *and* meteorites. *Identify key features of meteoroids, and then contrast meteors and meteorites.*

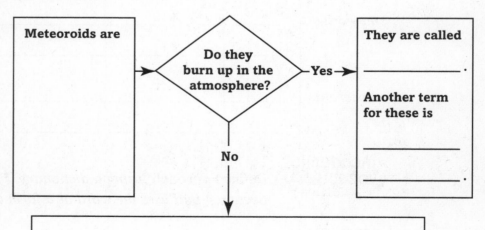

Meteoroids are

Do they burn up in the atmosphere?

Yes→ They are called _____ .

Another term for these is

_____

_____ .

No

They are called _____ . They come from

1. _____   2. _____

3. _____   4. _____

Section 4 Other Objects in the Solar System (continued)

| ◁ Main Idea ▷ | _____ ◁ Details ▷ _____ |

Asteroids

I found this information on page _____ .

Organize *information about asteroids. Complete the outline.*

Asteroids are _____

_____ .

A. Location

1. _____

2. _____

B. What scientists learn from asteroids

1. _____

2. _____

Model *the appearance of the asteroid belt in the solar system. Identify the two planets between which it lies.*

┌──┐
│   │
│   │
│   │
│   │
│   │
│   │
│   │
└──┘

┌─────────────────┐
│ **SYNTHESIZE IT** │ Compare and contrast comets, meteoroids, and asteroids in
│ **a paragraph or a chart.** │
└─────────────────┘

The Solar System Chapter Wrap-Up

Now that you have read the chapter, think about what you have learned and complete the table below. Compare your previous answers with these.

1. Write an **A** if you agree with the statement.
2. Write a **D** if you disagree with the statement.

The Solar System	After You Read
• The planets revolve around Earth.	
• The solar system is more than 4.6 billion years old.	
• Mercury has an atmosphere similar to Earth's.	
• Uranus has craters and deep valleys.	
• Earth is the only planet known to be able to support life.	

Review

Use this checklist to help you study.

☐ Review the information you included in your Foldable.

☐ Study your *Science Notebook* on this chapter.

☐ Study the definitions of vocabulary words.

☐ Review daily homework assignments.

☐ Re-read the chapter and review the charts, graphs, and illustrations.

☐ Review the Self Check at the end of each section.

☐ Look over the Chapter Review at the end of the chapter.

SUMMARIZE IT

You are planning a new space probe mission to the solar system. Decide on one or more planets, moons, comets, or asteroids that you would like to study. Explain what you expect to see and learn about each object.

_____

_____

_____

_____

Stars and Galaxies

Before You Read

Before you read the chapter, respond to these statements.

1. Write an **A** if you agree with the statement.

2. Write a **D** if you disagree with the statement.

Before You Read	Stars and Galaxies
	• Modern astronomy divides the sky into 88 constellations.
	• The Sun is an ordinary star and is the center of our solar system.
	• All stars have the same brightness.
	• The Milky Way is a part of a cluster called the Local Group, made up of about 45 galaxies.

Construct the Foldable as directed at the beginning of this chapter.

Science Journal

Write a description in your Science Journal of a galaxy.

_____

_____

_____

_____

_____

_____

_____

Stars and Galaxies
Section 1 Stars

Predict *three topics that will be discussed in Section 1 as you scan the headings and illustrations.*

1. _____

2. _____

3. _____

Review Vocabulary

Define star *to show its scientific meaning.*

star

_____

_____

New Vocabulary

Define the following terms to show their scientific meanings.

constellation

_____

_____

absolute magnitude

_____

_____

apparent magnitude

_____

_____

light-year

_____

_____

Academic Vocabulary

Use a dictionary to define component *as a noun. Then explain what the statement "breaking it down into its component parts" might mean.*

component

_____

_____

Section 1 Stars (continued)

Main Idea	Details

Constellations

I found this information on page _____.

Organize *facts about* constellations *into an outline. Use the structure provided below as a guide.*

   I. Constellations

      A. _____

         _____

      B. _____

         _____

      C. _____

         _____

   II. Movement of constellations

      A. Circumpolar constellations

         1. _____

            _____

         2. _____

            _____

      B. Other constellations

         1. _____

            _____

         2. _____

            _____

Absolute and Apparent Magnitudes

I found this information on page _____.

Complete *the diagram to show how each type of* magnitude *is related to a star's distance.*

Effect of Distance on Magnitude	→	Absolute magnitude _____
	→	Apparent magnitude _____

Section 1 Stars (continued)

Main Idea

Details

Measurement in Space

I found this information on page _____.

Analyze *the diagram below that shows how* parallax *occurs as Earth moves in its orbit.*

Background of distant stars

A
Star A has a small parallax

B
Star B has a large parallax

Lines of sight from Earth to star A

Lines of sight from Earth to star B

Earth in January

Earth in July

Properties of Stars

I found this information on page _____.

Summarize *how astronomers use parallax.*

_____

_____

_____

_____

Sequence *the colors of stars by temperature. Complete the diagram by writing the correct color in each box.*

Temperature	Cooler	Medium	Hotter
Star Color			

SYNTHESIZE IT

A hot, blue-white star has brighter absolute magnitude than a cooler, red star. The red star appears brighter from Earth. What can you conclude about the two stars?

_____

_____

Stars and Galaxies
Section 2 The Sun

Skim *through Section 2 of your book. Write three questions that come to mind from reading the headings and examining the illustrations.*

1. _____

2. _____

3. _____

Review Vocabulary

Define cycle *to show its scientific meaning.*

cycle _____

_____

New Vocabulary

Write a sentence from your book in which each term appears.

photosphere _____

_____

chromosphere _____

_____

corona _____

_____

sunspots _____

_____

Academic Vocabulary

Use a dictionary to define nuclear *to show its scientific meaning.* Use nuclear *in an original sentence.*

nuclear _____

_____

Section 2 The Sun (continued)

| **Main Idea** | **Details** |

The Sun's Layers

I found this information on page _____.

Summarize *basic information about the Sun. Complete the graphic organizer.*

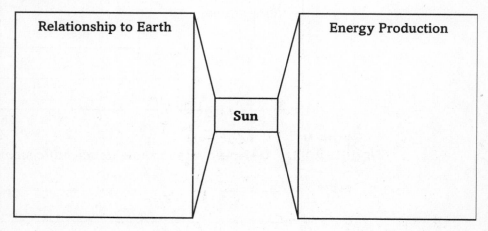

Relationship to Earth

Sun

Energy Production

The Sun's Atmosphere

I found this information on page _____.

Model *the Sun, including the following features. Include captions summarizing each feature.*

- chromosphere
- convection zone
- core
- corona
- photosphere
- radiation zone

Section 2 The Sun (continued)

Main Idea

Surface Features

*I found this information
on page _____.*

The Sun—An
Average Star

*I found this information
on page _____.*

Details

Organize *information about the Sun's surface features.*

Sunspots: _____

_____

_____

Prominences: _____

_____

_____

Flares: _____

_____

_____

Coronal mass ejection (CME): _____

_____

_____

Compare and contrast *the Sun with other stars. Complete the
paragraph below.*

   Compared with other stars, the Sun's _____, _____

_____, and _____ are about average. In contrast with

other stars, the Sun _____

and _____ .

CONNECT IT

Choose one characteristic you have learned about the Sun, such as
its size, structure, or distance from Earth. Suppose that the characteristic was different.
Predict how this would affect life on Earth.

_____

_____

_____

Stars and Galaxies
Section 3 Evolution of Stars

Scan *the headings of Section 3 to find three stages of the evolution of stars.*

1. _____ 2. _____ 3. _____

Review Vocabulary

Define gravity. *Use the term in a sentence to show its scientific meaning.*

gravity

_____

_____

New Vocabulary

Define the following terms. Write a sentence to show each term's scientific meaning.

nebula

_____

_____

_____

_____

white dwarf

_____

_____

_____

neutron star

_____

_____

_____

_____

Academic Vocabulary

Define enormous *using a dictionary.*

enormous

_____

_____

Section 3 Evolution of Stars (continued)

Main Idea	Details

Classifying Stars

I found this information on page _____.

Classify *stars using the H-R diagram. Label the diagram below to show where you would expect to find* white dwarfs, *the* main sequence, supergiants, giants, *and the* Sun.

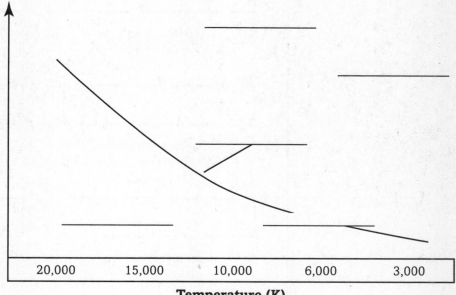

increasing brightness

Temperature (K)

Spectra Class
O   B   A   F G   K M

How do stars shine?

I found this information on page _____.

Summarize *how stars generate energy.*

_____

_____

_____

_____

_____

_____

Section 3 Evolution of Stars (continued)

Main Idea	Details

Evolution of Stars

I found this information on page _____ .

Sequence *the evolution of stars. Complete the flow chart.*

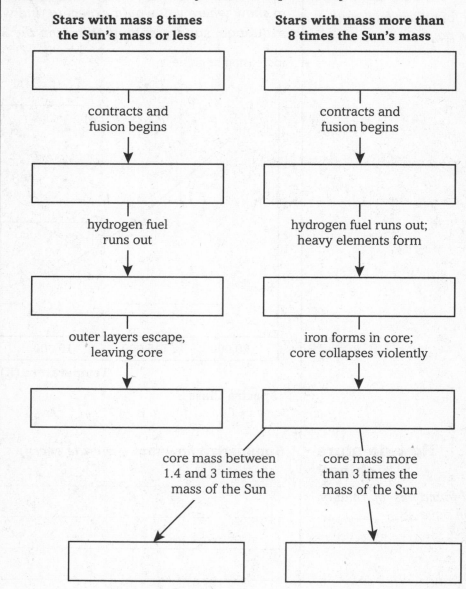

Stars with mass 8 times
the Sun's mass or less

contracts and
fusion begins

hydrogen fuel
runs out

outer layers escape,
leaving core

core mass between
1.4 and 3 times the
mass of the Sun

Stars with mass more than
8 times the Sun's mass

contracts and
fusion begins

hydrogen fuel runs out;
heavy elements form

iron forms in core;
core collapses violently

core mass more
than 3 times the
mass of the Sun

CONNECT IT Evaluate why supernovas are important to the existence of life on Earth.

_____

_____

_____

Stars and Galaxies
Section 4 Galaxies and the Universe

Preview *Section 4 of your book using the list below.*

☐ Read all section headings.

☐ Read all bold words.

☐ Look at all of the pictures.

☐ Think about what you already know about galaxies and the universe.

Write two facts that you discovered during your preview.

1. _____

2. _____

Review Vocabulary

Define universe *to reflect its scientific meaning.*

universe

_____

New Vocabulary

Define the following key terms. Then write sentences to show the scientific meaning of each term.

galaxy

_____

_____

_____

_____

big bang theory

_____

_____

_____

_____

Academic Vocabulary

Define normal. *Write a sentence to show its scientific meaning.*

normal

_____

_____

Section 4 Galaxies and the Universe (continued)

| Main Idea | Details |

Galaxies

I found this information on page _____.

Classify *the three major types* of galaxies. *Complete the chart.*

Galaxy Type	Description
	Spiral arms that wind outward from the center
	Does not look like the other two types of galaxies; many possible shapes

The Milky Way

I found this information on page _____.

Model *the Milky Way galaxy.*

- Draw a side view and overhead view of the Milky Way.

- Mark the Sun's position on both views.

- Label the size of the Milky Way and the distance from the center to the Sun's position on the overhead view.

Side view	Overhead view

Identify *three other facts about the Milky Way.*

_____

_____

_____

_____

Section 4 Galaxies and the Universe (continued)

Main Idea	**Details**

Origin of the Universe

I found this information on page _____.

Contrast *two models of the origin of the universe: the steady state theory and the oscillating model.*

Steady state theory: _____

_____

Oscillating model: _____

_____

Expansion of the Universe

I found this information on page _____.

Analyze *how scientists used the Doppler shift to reach a conclusion about whether the universe is expanding or contracting.*

 Observation

 Conclusion

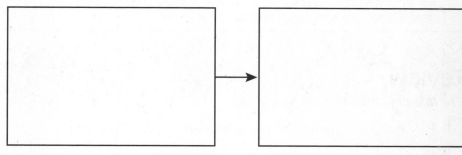

The Big Bang Theory

I found this information on page _____.

Summarize *the big bang theory of the origin of the universe.*

_____

_____

_____

_____

_____

SUMMARIZE IT

Describe your location in the universe as completely as you can.

_____

_____

_____

_____

Stars and Galaxies Chapter Wrap-Up

*Now that you have read the chapter, think about what you have learned and complete
the table below. Compare your previous answers with these.*

    1. Write an **A** if you agree with the statement.

    2. Write a **D** if you disagree with the statement.

Stars and Galaxies	After You Read
• Modern astronomy divides the sky into 88 constellations.	
• The Sun is an ordinary star and is the center of our solar system.	
• All stars have the same brightness.	
• The Milky Way is a part of a cluster called the Local Group, made up of about 45 galaxies.	

Review

Use this checklist to help you study.

☐ Review the information you included in your Foldable.

☐ Study your *Science Notebook* on this chapter.

☐ Study the definitions of vocabulary words.

☐ Review daily homework assignments.

☐ Re-read the chapter and review the charts, graphs, and illustrations.

☐ Review the Self Check at the end of each section.

☐ Look over the Chapter Review at the end of the chapter.

SUMMARIZE IT After reading this chapter, identify three things that you have
learned about stars and galaxies.

_____

_____

_____

_____

accompany: to go together with; to happen at the same time as

accumulate: to gather, pile up, or collect

accurate: careful and exact; without mistakes or errors

affect: to influence

approach: to come near

area: particular space, region, or section

chemical: any substance used in or obtained by a chemical process

collapse: to fall or shrink together abruptly and completely

compensate: to make up for

component: part of a machine or system

consist: to be made up of; to contain

constant: not changing; remaining the same; remaining free of variation; regular; stable

contract: to make or become shorter or smaller

controversy: argument or debate

convert: to change from one form to another form

core: center; a central part of something

create: to bring about

cycle: series of actions that repeat

derive: to get or receive from a source

detect: to discover something hidden or not easily noticed

diverse: not all the same, varied

emerge: to come out; to appear

enormous: having great size

environment: the physical, chemical, and biotic factors that surround living things

erode: to wear away

eventual: ultimately resulting

exceed: to go beyond or be greater than

expose: to leave open or without protection; to reveal

extract: to take, get, or pull out

formula: a group of symbols and figures showing the elements in a chemical compound

goal: objective or end that one strives to achieve

hypothesis: a reasonable guess that can be tested and is based on what is known and what is observed

impact: a strong effect

indicate: to be or give a sign of

infer: to arrive at a conclusion or an opinion by reasoning

interval: space or time between events

layer: one thickness over another

likewise: in the same way

locate: to find the position or site of

maintain: to continue; to support

normal: conforming to a type; standard or regular pattern

nuclear: of or relating to the atomic nucleus

Academic Vocabulary

objective: open and fair; without bias

obtain: to get through effort; gain

obvious: easy to see or understand; clear

occur: to happen or take place

outcome: end result of a particular situation or experiment

parallel: being the same distance apart at all points

phenomenon: any fact, condition, or happening that can be observed and described in a scientific way

physical: having to do with things we experience through our senses

predict: to tell what one thinks will happen in the future

process: series of changes by which something develops

range: the difference between the highest and lowest values

ratio: relation of one thing to another in size or amount

recover: to get back something that has been lost

release: to set free or let go

reveal: to make known; to show or display

reverse: to go in the opposite direction

rigid: not bending or moving; stiff and hard

role: part played by a person or thing

sequence: one thing following another in a fixed order

stress: a force exerted when one body presses on, pulls on, pushes against, or tends to compress or twist another body

structure: anything that is built; a home or other building or a molecule's structure

sum: the number that results when two or more numbers are added

survey: to look at or study in detail

survive: to continue to exist; to live through

technology: use of science for practical purposes, especially in engineering and industry

trace: a very small amount

transfer: to move, carry, send, or change from one person or place to another

transform: to change the nature or condition of something

transport: to carry from one place to another

undergo: to go through; to endure

underlie: to lie beneath

vary: to change; to make different

visible: able to be seen; perceptible with the eye

volume: the amount of space taken up by an object or substance